SUNDAY DINNER

A Novel

Ben Cardinale

Statue of Liberty

Give me your tired, your poor,

Your huddled masses yearning to breathe free,

The wretched refuse of your teeming shore.

Send these, the homeless, tempest tossed to me,

I lift my lamp besides the golden door!

Emma Lazarus (1883)

DEDICATION

To Martha Cardinale
Whose love blessed all her children
Thanks, Mom for all the meals.

Kitchen closed.

Preface

I've often been asked why it was so special growing up in the 1950's and 60's in Bensonhurst, a working-class neighborhood in Brooklyn. The main reason I've come up with is we grew up with three distinct generations. Firstly, Jewish grandparents from Europe and Syria and Italian grandparents from Sicily. Secondly, our parents who were born here, becoming Tom Brokaw's Greatest Generation. And thirdly, us, the Silent Generation. Each generation bringing their values and conversation to a dinner table where we ate mouthwatering, ethnic food cooked by our mothers and grandmothers. We became a blend of all of them. We combined our grandparents love of family, our parents love of country and for us, our love of self. Each generation more Americanized than the one before. More educated. More worldly. More adventurous. But it was that combination of the three that made us who we are today. The best of us, patriotic, loyal, and decent.

It was a simpler time. Nobody locked their doors; your sister could come home late at night and not worry about her safety. We hung out in the streets together because there was no social media to divert our attention. We lived in crowded apartment buildings and three family houses with no air conditioning which made our street forays a necessity. We survived by always being with groups of friends to support and protect us. Stickball, triangle, stoopball, jacks, hopscotch, games passed down from big brother to little brother and big sister to little sister. If you did something wrong somebody's mother, Mrs. Goldberg, would tell your mother, Mrs. Cardinale, about it. Ethnicity didn't matter. We had wealthy and middle-class neighbors. But we all went to the same public schools There was no wealth divide. Nobody thought they were better than anyone else.

We respected authority – parents, religious leaders, teachers, coaches, and cops even if they sometimes didn't deserve it. We gave people the benefit of the doubt. I'm going to love and respect you until you give me a reason not to.

Sunday Dinner is one story of a boy coming of age in a Jewish/Italian neighborhood in Brooklyn. There are so many others.

CONTENTS

1   Make Room for Daddy   1

2   Star of David   23

3   Creditors Come Calling   59

4   A Man Needs to Sweat to Feel Good   89

5   Reaching Second Base   121

6   Coming of Age   151

7   Saddle Up the Horses   191

8   Trouble in Paradise   217

9   The Final Curtain   255

Chapter 1
Make Room for Daddy

Author at 10

I grew up in the 50's and 60's in a three-family brick house in Bensonhurst, a working-class neighborhood in Brooklyn. This house spoke of permanence and tradition, much like the people who inhabited it. The neighborhood was composed of European and Syrian Jews and us Italians. The European Jews lived in six story apartment buildings. The Syrian Jews lived in two and three family houses. We Italians lived mainly in three family houses. Usually a grandparent owned the house and lived on the ground floor and rented for practically nothing the two upstairs apartments to their grown children or other close family members. The compound we called it. Why the European Jews rented small apartments in big buildings didn't make sense since they had a lot more money than the rest of us. But my best friend, Howie Schwartz explained it to me.

"See, after what happened to us in the pogroms, we always have to be ready to pack up quickly and get out of town. It's a lot easier to do from a small apartment than a house."

Almost all the women were homemakers. The Jewish men had jobs like salesman, druggist, store owner and the Italians were all in the trades. Carpenters, plumbers, electricians and brick layers. The Jewish men showered before work and the Italian men after. But the best thing Bensonhurst had going for it was the food. I loved the Jewish pastrami sandwiches, pickles and potato knishes, and the Arabic stuffed grape leaves with apricots and torpedo kibbehs, but for my money the Italian food was the best. Friday nights and Saturdays the Jews would celebrate Shabbat, but the Italians had Sunday. Yup, Sunday was all ours. Sunday dinner was our time to shine. The one constant for every Italian family if you don't count yelling, was food. Homemade

2

food. Unforgettable food. Smell–it-halfway-down-the-block food.

While my grandfather was the undisputed head of the family, my grandmother was its center. She ruled the roost through our digestive systems. And every Sunday she made this incredible dinner. I looked forward to it. It marked the end of my week. Only the family. It was always held downstairs in her apartment. Always.

I was almost sixteen at the time, and I was on my way to the local grocery store to get a few loaves of Italian bread for dinner. Joe and Josie's, a brother and sister establishment, although everyone thought they were husband and wife. Joe worked the back with the boxes, Josie worked the front with the customers. Josie had these strange looking eyebrows that were penciled in way above her eyes making her look like she came from outer space. Maybe she did, I never saw her birth certificate. The store was the size of a postage stamp but had fresh food. I entered the store and heard the tinkle of a tiny bell announce my arrival. Their security system. I picked out bread from the bin. I took my goods to the checkout, where Josie, an oversized carpenter's pencil in hand, was at the ready. On a large brown paper bag, she tallied what I owed. Cinque, otto, mumble, mumble. $1.88. I gave her 2 bucks and she rang me up. She smiled at me, having forgiven me from riding my bike over some freshly poured concrete in front of the store. I smiled back, waved goodbye to Joe in the back and left.

I headed up 73rd street because there was a mean dog on 72nd named Lucky, which is what you were if you didn't meet up with him. Plus, it was prettier on 73rd. Maple trees formed a chorus line on each side of the street that would make the Rockettes jealous. As I passed houses and alleys, I could hear the soulful Yiddish song, *Shalom Aleichem* coming from somebody's record player. A few houses down the voice of Jerry Vale sang the Italian ballad, *Inamorata*. A few more houses the Sephardic song *Adon Olam* wafted up into the morning air. Those songs mirrored the three distinct ethnic groups represented in Bensonhurst. I peeked in on an elderly Italian woman hanging her undergarments unashamedly on a clothesline. I passed Mr. Melcher and Mr. Weinstein playing chess. It was Mr. Weinstein's turn. It was always Mr. Weinstein's turn, much to the dismay of Mr. Melcher. I kept on going and breezed by a line of Jewish women sitting on folding chairs in front of their apartment building guarding their turf. A lack of air conditioners chased them outside where they formed their own social club. They were the town criers. "Look Mildred he brings bread for dinner. Every Sunday. What a good boy." I tried sneaking by two Italian girls teasing their hair to mountaintop heights.

"I'm telling you, Marie, if Vinny 'aks' me to marry him I'm saying yes. Strike while the iron is hot. Right?"

"Right. Plus, he already has a good job. Carpet installation. Everybody needs carpeting. Oh hi, Joey," Marie said. "You have my phone number; how come you haven't called?"

"I have a girlfriend, Marie," I told her for the umpteenth time.

"That Jewish girl, you still with her? She carries a backpack full of books. She'll be hunchback before she's eighteen. Whatsamatter 'ascared' to go out with a real woman?"

Damn right I was 'ascared.' Italian girls made me nervous. They were way more sexually advanced than the Jewish girls. They wanted to be married by eighteen, have kids right away and move in with their parents. Not the life path I had in mind. I arrived at my house. Two pink flamingoes graced our front lawn flanking a white Magnolia tree. Not sure what significance pink flamingoes had in Italian American folklore, but they were the decoration of choice for many Italian homes. I headed to the backyard through an alley that separated my house from my neighbor. The backyard had a vegetable garden with raised beds that my grandmother tended and a large fig tree that was my grandfather's domain.

My grandfather, Vince Palumbo was in his woodshop. His man cave. I stopped in to say hello. My grandfather was planning on my coming into the business. He would show me an old photograph that hung in his shop of a man standing proudly with an eighteen-year-old boy in front of a sign, "Palumbo & Sons Construction."

"Joey, when my father brought me to this country, he didn't speak a word of English. All he had was one suit and a strong back. He began as a laborer digging ditches. Then he worked his way up to apprentice carpenter, then journeyman, then master carpenter. He saved his money and started Palumbo Construction. And when I turned eighteen, he brought me into the business. And when your father and uncle turned eighteen, I brought them into the business. Son after son. After son. And when you turn eighteen, I'm going to bring you into the business. Family. That's all that matters. Capisce?"

I didn't have the heart to tell him that although I liked construction, I was thinking I'd like to do something else, career wise. Maybe be a writer.

"Capisce," I said and left it at that.

I went inside to the kitchen and handed the loaves of bread to my grandmother, Angela. Reputed to be the best cook in the family. My grandparent's bottom apartment was long and narrow. The interior had dark mahogany furniture. Pictures of Joe DiMaggio and Pope Paul VI graced the walls in their dining room. Two giant mermaid candles were displayed on the table when we weren't eating, which wasn't very often. All lamp shades, stuffed chairs and couch were covered in clear plastic. It did its job of keeping people off of them. Especially in the summer. Shvitz city

Before dinner my grandmother set the table. She'd start off by putting out two decanters of homemade red burgundy wine and several bottles of Canada Dry ginger ale. Then a few pitchers of tap water, and a bottle of sparkling Pellegrino mineral water.

"You want the plain or the fancy?" she would ask.

Most people chose the plain. It was who we were.

She had antipasto as an appetizer. Rolled up salami slices, roasted red peppers, chunks of provolone, black olives, and olive oil on top. Then she changed plates. Second course was macaroni or ravioli. Always with freshly made red tomato sauce. No Ragu allowed in this house. And then she changed plates again. Main course was usually ham, roast beef, chicken, pork, or lamb, you name it she had it. She also had mashed potatoes and zucchini, spinach, or asparagus. And she changed plates again. Then out came the salad. Iceberg lettuce, no exotic here, and sliced white onions. And she changed plates. Next she had fruit and nuts on paper plates because she ran out of real ones. Usually pears, sometimes peaches cut up and immersed in red wine. The nuts were walnuts or pecans in their shells, so you had to crack them open yourself with a nutcracker. Or ask my Uncle Tommy to do it for you. And last, if they could still move, the grownups had coffee or espresso with anisette and some homemade cannolis for dessert. I had milk and Yankee Doodles, my homage to the New World.

My grandmother was the glue that kept the family together. A very sweet woman, except if someone came to her door on a Sunday.

"Hello, would you like the latest edition of the Encyclopedia Britannica?" a salesman would ask.

"Sorry, we're eating!" she'd bark out and slam the door. Then she'd head back to the stove cursing in Italian, "Mannaggia,"

The dining room table was rectangular and with three extensions seated a maximum of twelve. Five, five and two at the ends. One of my chores was to put the extensions in. I got pretty good at it. I could line up the pegs and holes with my eyes closed. The table filled the room. It was tight, but warm and comforting. After the leaves were in, I put the chairs in place. My grandfather always sat at the head. I sat at his right. A seat of immense importance I was told. My grandmother sat next to the kitchen. Aunt Jenny sat next to her to help. She was the family saint, always looking out for others. But in the neighborhood, a zitellona. Unmarried. A big sin in Italian homes if you were a woman over thirty.

When my mother, Gina wasn't holding an open house she sat in the middle, facing the windows. She had just started working in 'The Real Estate,' my family's moniker for a real estate agent. Not sure where the 'The' came from. Maybe it was the same guy who named the apartment building on Bay Parkway, 'The Le Parc.' 'Le' means 'the' in French. What a beauty she was. Dark brown hair, hourglass figure, perfect olive skin. At open school week she'd come meet my teachers. What a commotion she made with the boys.

"That's Joey's mother? Get out of here. I'd like to..." This was usually followed by an arm pumping gesture. She could sing, too. At family gatherings, weddings, and funerals. Her 'Ave Maria' would make grown men cry. Little boys, too. Things gone another way she might've made it big in show business.

Uncle Tommy sat at the other end. He worked with my grandfather in the family construction business. He had polio as a child and walked with a severe limp. He had this enormous upper body from lifting weights, and he could crush walnuts in his bare hands. Jonas Salk had just discovered a cure for polio, so you had to feel sorry for him for being born a few years too early.

There was also Uncle Frankie. He lived in the basement. He didn't go into the family business because he was afraid to leave the house. He had a mild form of agoraphobia, although at the time we didn't have a name for it. We just said he was potz. Crazy. The Brooklyn word for all things mental. Uncle Joe used to call him, "The Rats." Not the singular "The Rat" which would have made more sense. He painted with oils. The Madonna and Child his forever subject. He wore a tattered looking brown cap all the time. I mean all the time. For all I know he might have showered in it. Anyway, late in life my Uncle Sal got him a job at the Steeplechase Amusement Park in Coney Island. The job was to push the button to blow air up ladies' dresses as they exited the Haunted House ride. Like the famous Marilyn Monroe photo. Not brain surgery, my uncle soon got the hang of it. He would come upstairs on Sunday to eat with us. He sat next to me, and sometimes he ate out of my plate just to tease me. But I didn't mind. I just ate out of his plate.

And of course, there was Aunt Theresa. God bless her. She sat as far away from the kitchen as possible. "God forbid she should lift a finger," my grandfather used to say. Aunt Theresa lived alone in the upstairs rear apartment of our house. She always dressed in black. It wasn't the same dress, mind you, she had seven of them. One for each day. She walked ten blocks to St. Athanasius church every morning, rain or shine. She was still mourning the death of her husband, Eddie, who died fifteen years ago. I never met the man, but he must have been quite a guy to get that kind of devotion. But my grandmother felt sorry for her sister. An old lady surrounded by family but all alone.

My grandmother's brother, Uncle Sal was sometimes there. He had moved to Staten Island. He was part of the beginning of the Great Italian Exodus. The more adventurous European Jews had begun moving to Long Island. The wealthier Syrian Jews started moving to Ocean Parkway, then Deal, New Jersey. But an Italian moving out of Brooklyn was the biggest sin of all. At least to my grandfather. "Nothing is impossible as long as the family sticks together," he always said.

Uncle Sal built tract houses in Staten Island. My grandfather said he was in the Mafia. "Where do you think he got the cash to buy the land for these houses?"

He was probably right. But it didn't matter much to the rest of the family. Me especially. Uncle Sal would give me a hundred-dollar bill when he came over.

"Here's a little something, take your girl out. Shh, nobody has to know," he'd whisper.

And I forgave him for all his past and future transgressions. Anyway, some Sundays he'd make the one-hour trek into Brooklyn. He had recently married Bernice, a sweet young platinum blonde. She didn't say much. I thought the family overwhelmed her. Not surprising they could overwhelm anybody.

I was especially looking forward to this Sunday's dinner. The first Sunday my father was back home from Vietnam. My father wore his army uniform to the table that day. My grandmother insisted. He sat to the right of my grandfather. I sat in that place while my dad was overseas, but he was home now, and would regain his place as my grandfather's right-hand man.

My grandparents adored my dad. Everybody did. He was called Baby Danny when he was well a baby. Actually, they called him baby Danny when he got older. Sometimes Baby Danny Ma-*ma* if you can believe it. It was hard to believe my father could kill anyone, Viet Cong or not. He never got angry. I always thought of him as a gentle man living in a harsh world.

I watched my father that day at the table. He seemed so uncomfortable, as if he'd been through too much to be enjoying such a common pleasure. This was before PTSD; post-traumatic stress disorder was identified. Looking back this was what he must have had.

After my grandmother brought out the huge plate of antipasto to start dinner the family all clasped hands and waited, all eyes on the cuckoo clock. At precisely two o'clock the cuckoo emerged, the signal for my grandmother to do the dinner prayer.

"Bless us Oh Lord and these Thy gifts which we are about to receive from Thy bounty through Christ our Lord." Then she added, "And thank you for bringing Danny home to us, where he belongs. Amen."

Amens, cheering, banging utensils on glasses.

"Enough already, let's eat," my father said.

The family began passing the antipasto plate around. When the plate got to Uncle Tommy, he reached for it and knocked over his red burgundy wine all over the white tablecloth. "Oops." This was a common occurrence by my uncle. With meat hooks for hands he had trouble handling delicate things. Rather than change the tablecloth my grandmother put a large white napkin over the stain. A veteran move by her.

But the thing I remember most about Sunday dinners was the conversation. The dinner talk was lively, sometimes contentious, always memorable. But lately the mood was somber. Palumbo & Sons was in a slump and it cast a pall over the Sunday dinners. The talk was mostly dominated by my grandfather and it was almost always about the good old days in construction.

But this day I hoped would be different. My father had just come home a few days ago. We had something else to talk about. Something bigger. Worldly. But, unfortunately, it didn't quite work out that way.

"Everything's changed, Danny. People don't appreciate good work anymore," my grandfather complained.

"Right, everything's changed," my father agreed.

"It's not like the old days, Danny. People used to wait months for us. A good job at a fair price," my grandfather went on. "Now we have to almost beg for work. Everything's changed, Danny. Everything."

Uncle Sal nudged my father, trying to rescue him. He showed him a photo of a sprawling ranch style home.

"Beautiful, heh? Got a lap pool in my backyard that's all fenced in. I can swim nude if I want to."

Bernice elbowed him.

"Not that I want to," Uncle Sal quickly added.

"I gotta come visit, Sal," Uncle Frankie said.

Uncle Frankie would sooner grow two heads than leave the basement.

"Sure, say the word I'll come get you. Gina loves it out there. Don't you, Gina?"

"I do. You get a lot for your money. And space. Lots of space," my mother said.

"I'd like to come visit, maybe I can find a good man there. Or any man for that matter, I'm not particular," Aunt Jenny chimed in.

"How's the pastry? Do they have 'Luigi Alba's'? I gotta have my 'Luigi Alba's'," Aunt Theresa wondered.

"Who needs 'Luigi Alba's' when you have supermarkets with their own bakeries. Besides, we eat healthy. Alfalfa sprouts, soybeans, avocados."

"Avocados. Wow," Aunt Theresa exclaimed, then whispered to Bernice, "What's an avocado?"

"It's a dark green pear-shaped fruit but it tastes awful. Sal loves them," Bernice whispered back.

"My company opened an office there. They say Staten Island is the new Promised Land," my mother added.

Uh oh. The magic words. Promised Land. That could set my grandfather off.

"What Promised Land? It's the suburbs. You have to drive everywhere. Mile after mile of tract housing. Who needs it?" he exclaimed.

"Obviously a lot of people. I can't build them fast enough," Uncle Sal needled back.

"You put some sticks together and call that a house?"

"I build nothing but quality. You're jealous because I have more work than you."

"Are you saying I don't have work?"

"Who said that? I didn't say that. Did I say that?"

And with that a full-scale argument ensued.

"See what you missed," I whispered to my father.

My father looked off in the distance.

"Are you okay, Dad?" I asked.

"Huh? Yeah, sure," he said. And then he snapped back to attention.

I could see my father wasn't the same. But in this family if you didn't talk about it, you didn't have a problem. So, no one in the family had a problem.

After dinner the women cleaned up while the men went into the living room and smoked cigars. De Nobili Toscana Longs. They stunk the place up. I couldn't believe anybody could actually enjoy them, but the men seemed to as they rolled them around in their mouths.

Later everybody went outside to the curb to say goodbye. Uncle Sal did his usual honk twice, then he sped off in his new Cadillac convertible. A final dig at my grandfather and an end to another Sunday dinner.

After dinner I went upstairs to my apartment. The staircase that led upstairs sloped to the right. You had to hold the banister tightly to keep from losing your balance. At least the adults did. I was able to bound up those stairs three steps at a time. I considered it part of my basketball training. I thought about my father. It had to be a temporary condition. He had a family that loved him, a business that needed him. What more could a man want? Besides I was starting my final year in junior high and I wasn't exactly knocking it out of the ballpark.

For one thing I slept in the living room. Not what a boy my age aspired to. My bed was a Castro convertible sofa which I had to open every night and close every morning. It was advertised on TV. A little girl opened the bed and they played this jingle.

"Who was the first to conquer space? It's incontrovertible! That the first to conquer living space is a Castro Convertible! Who conquered space with fine design? Who saves you money all the time? Who's tops in the convertible line? Castro Convertible!"

I heard that maddening jingle in my head every time I opened or closed that stupid bed. And the mattress was the pits. Any mattress that had to be folded by necessity had to be too soft. I considered myself somewhat of a connoisseur of mattresses. I used to help deliver them for Uncle Joe on 20th Avenue. "Garofalo Bedding," perhaps you've heard of them. Ninety percent of all mattresses in Bensonhurst came from Uncle Joe's store. European Jews, Syrian Jews, Italians, everyone. I thought that was what bound us all together, we all slept on a Garofalo mattress.

Our apartment was in the front. It was tiny. 800 square feet. Tops. The bathroom was so small when you opened the door you hit the sink. So, I squeezed in and washed my hands. It was the pedestal kind, small, you had to be careful not to have the water splash all over the tile floor. But it did. Always.

The kitchen was tiny, too. There was almost no counter space other than the top of the stove. A Blackstone washing machine was somehow squeezed in there, and it was my job to drag the hose over to the sink and hook it up to the faucet. Funny you'd think a house full of builders would have corrected these problems. Afraid to open a 'can of worms,' they'd say.

The front apartment was preferred over the back because you at least could look down on the street. That was a big plus except when the garbage trucks showed up six-thirty Monday mornings. Two men would come get the metal cans carefully placed by you in the alley, drag them to the truck parked in the street, dump the garbage in the truck while it made this loud rrring sound. Then they'd drag the cans back and toss them in place, not even close to where you left them. It was as if they were punishing customers for crimes against humanity.

I could've slept in the second bedroom after my great grandfather, Papa Nunzio, the founder of Palumbo & Sons Construction had died creating a vacancy. Papa Nunzio stayed with us and my mother took care of him. We all did. Papa would sit in his rocking chair looking out the window at people passing by, and I'd read the Italian newspaper to him, "*Il Progresso*". Towards the end of his life I didn't think Papa understood what I was reading but he liked to hear my voice. He probably had Alzheimer's. That was the everything disease in the neighborhood. Any lapse in memory that is what you had.

As Papa was being wheeled to the ambulance because he was having trouble breathing, he called me over and whispered in my ear, "Donna mess with the Effa B.I." I didn't know where he got that from. Papa used to watch 'The Untouchables' maybe that was it.

Papa never did reach the hospital, he died on the way. He was ninety-two. They had a wake at Graziano Funeral Home, a mass at St. Athanasius, followed by the burial at the Italian cemetery on McDonald Avenue. At each event there were less and less people. It was small to begin with since most of his brothers, sisters, and cousins had already died. I vowed that day that I didn't want to live that long, too lonely a way to go. Anyway, my mother needed an office for 'The Real Estate,' so I let her have the bedroom. She deserved it after all she did taking care of Papa. It was only fair. Fairness was everything in Brooklyn. I was considered a fair guy in the park. Everyone looked to me to choose up sides. They knew I wouldn't stack the sides so I would win. Some of the boys would try to influence me but I couldn't be bought. To this day I am driven to be fair. I consider it a vestige of growing up in Brooklyn. Fairness and loyalty our go-to revered traits.

After I opened the bed, I got my pillows and blankets out of the closet. My parents usually went to bed at the same time. Not so much that they wanted to, but with my bed out there was no place for them to go. I turned on the TV and watched one of my favorite shows, 'What's My Line?' with moderator, John Charles

Daly and panelists, Bennett Cerf, Arlene Francis and Dorothy Kilgallen. Sunday 10:30 to 11:00. A person would come on the show and write their occupation on a chalk board. An unusual one like lion tamer, goat herder, or astronaut. The panel would have to guess the occupation using questions that could only be answered 'yes' or 'no'. Ten no's and the game was over. I loved the show and it gave me ideas of what I might do, career wise. In another segment the panelists put on blindfolds and tried to guess the identity of a mystery guest. That night the secret guest was writer, Neil Simon. Almost everyone in Brooklyn watched the show. It officially ended the weekend. After the show you went straight to bed. I turned off the TV and waved goodnight to the next-door neighbor, Nathan Ozeri, through a second-floor window. Then I closed the blinds for privacy and got under the covers. I laid in bed thinking about my life. I loved my family, but I thought there might be more out there than what they had planned for me. I just had to go find it!

Chapter 2
Star of David

Seth Low Jr. High School

The school year had just begun at Seth Low Junior High School. In those days, junior high was seventh, eighth, and ninth grades. Then we went on to Lafayette High School for tenth, eleventh and twelfth. Education had its own meaning to the three cultural groups in the neighborhood. The Italian and Syrian kids were pressured to go to work after high school. But the European Jews, well it was a totally different story. They revered education. College was a must. They encouraged their kids to study. No, they demanded it.

Their kids were in classes 7-1, 8-1, 9-1. The lower the number the smarter the kids. Supposedly. The Syrian kids composed the mid numbers but us Italians brought up the rear. 7-14, 8-14, 9-14. Profiling they call it now, but back then nobody made a stink. The result was the European Jews had better books, better teachers and ultimately most went to college. But for us Italians college wasn't even a consideration. Books weren't cool, you could be accused of 'acting Jewish.' Besides what was the point? A bricklayer didn't need to know algebra. Just give him a string line, some bricks and mortar and he was set. And why on Earth did a carpenter need history? A hammer, yes, a measuring tape, yes, but history? Useless.

Even though I went to class with the Italian kids my mother told me to hang around the Jewish kids because they were going places. Without realizing it I took her advice. I played basketball for the Jewish Community House. My best friend and girlfriend were both Jewish. Howie Schwartz and Becky Fishbein. Every day we walked to Seth Low together. Howie and Becky lived in a majestic six story brick apartment building on Bay Parkway and 72nd street I mentioned earlier. The Le Parc. Apartments IB and 1C. Yup, next door neighbors.

I met Howie playing basketball in Seth Low Park. Howie's father was a family doctor, Samuel Schwartz. The kind of doctor you want. Caring, competent and Jewish. He was a God in my house. Forget Jesus. If they took a vote Dr. Schwartz would win. Hands down. When I was four, I got sick. Slight fever, a cough. My parents called in Dr. Genovese to care for me. He was the family doctor at the time and doctors made house calls in those days. Three bucks a visit plus seventy-five cents for a penicillin shot if it was needed. But the Palumbos were a healthy bunch for the most part, nothing serious had come up. Dr. Genovese gave me some pills, told me to drink lots of liquids and get plenty of rest. Seemed like sound advice. The problem was my condition was getting worse. Finally, when a fever reached 103 that was it. Forget Dr. Italian and go with Dr. Jew. In other words, Samuel Schwartz.

My father ran to The Le Parc slid across the polished marble lobby floor almost killing himself and knocked on the door of Apartment 1C. He waited. Finally, Becky's Dad, Si Fishbein, came to the door in his pajamas. Oops, wrong door. My father apologized profusely as Si signaled the Doc's next door. It happened a lot. My father knocked on 1B. Dr.

Schwartz answered the door. He was in his pajamas. Probably every man in the building was in his pajamas. Office hours were over a long time ago. No matter, he got himself dressed and came to my house right away. The amazing thing about Dr. Schwartz was he rarely needed to examine you. All he had to do was look at you. And he took one look at me and said: "This boy needs to go to the hospital immediately."

It turned out I had pleurisy pneumonia. Another few days I might've died. At least that's what people said. It was my first experience in a hospital. Dr. Schwartz visited me every day. So did my parents. The joke was when my parents were about to leave, I'd say in a sing song voice: "Don't-forget-to-come-tomorrow." And that became how the doctors and nurses referred to me, the 'Don't forget to come tomorrow boy.' It wasn't that I needed their support, it was because they'd bring food made by my grandmother. Meatball sandwiches, Italian sausage, homemade pizza, breaded veal cutlets, a couple of packages of Yankee Doodles slipped in. Hospital food was considered by my grandmother to be food from the 'outside,' to be avoided at all cost.

After a few weeks of IV drips and getting poked with needles I came home. The whole family was there and when I got out of the car they broke into applause. Dr. Schwartz clapping the loudest. My grandmother gave the doctor a tray of lasagna and sent him home. He had done enough.

You can imagine his standing in the house after that. You must understand this about Italians. You do something for us we are forever grateful. The bigger the thing the more grateful we are. Palumbo Construction remodeled Dr. Schwartz's office for practically nothing. And threw in new windows for Becky's bedroom.

I met Becky at the 'JCH', the Jewish Community House. Actually, I didn't meet her there, but I first saw her there. Howie and I had joined the Boy Scouts together and they held their meetings in a little room by the gym. There was this inside door that was always locked. It was against a side wall. One time we got there early, and someone tried the door. It opened. Turns out it opened to a hallway connecting the girls locker room to the pool. We had hit pay dirt! We turned off the lights in the meeting room and opened the door a crack and watched the young girls changing into their gym clothes. First the Eagle Scouts got a peek, then the First class, then the Second class, then us Tenderfoots. We flipped a coin. Heads. Howie went first.

"Wow, Joe, this is unbelievable!" he said.

"C'mon, before they all go home," I pleaded.

"And you didn't want to join the Boy Scouts?" Howie kept reminding me.

"Okay, okay, I was wrong. Let me see."

Finally, Howie relented.

"Take a gander, my paisano," Howie said.

I peeked. And that's when I saw Becky for the first time. It was love at first sight. Not because she was a ten, which she was, but because of the way she carried herself, with such confidence and poise. The next day one of the goody-two-shoes Eagle Scouts found it necessary to report us, so that ended that.

After that I'd see Becky at school, carrying a backpack full of books. One day I summoned the courage and went over to her.

"Uh Becky. Hi. You probably don't know me, I'm Joey Palumbo. I've seen you around. You know, around school. At Seth Low Park. The 'J'. In the gym at the 'J'. No place else at the 'J.' Just the gym. Anyway, you're probably busy but if not, maybe we could go to the Marboro this Saturday. To a movie. At the Marlboro."

"Sure, sounds like fun," she said happily.

"Huh?" I said, not believing what I just heard.

"I'd love to. What's playing?" she asked.

"The Cincinnati Kid, starring Steve McQueen."

"Sounds good," she said. "I love Steve McQueen."

"Great. I'll pick you up at noon. I mean I'll walk over to your house and pick you up. I don't have a car. But my birthday is coming up soon, so I'll be able to drive. Soon. But not yet."

Then it happened. Something I'd remember the rest of my life. She leaned over and gave me a kiss on the cheek.

"I was hoping you'd ask me out," she said sweetly.

"Really?"

"Really," she said.

I could hardly believe it. The smart, very popular, Becky Fishbein, no, the incredibly popular Becky Fishbein was going out with me, Joey Palumbo. A smart Jew in class 9-1 and a 'dumb' Italian in class 9-14. A miracle at the school on a par with Jesus walking on water. Or Moses parting the Red Sea.

We went out on our first date. I brought flowers to her house, a big hit with Mrs. Fishbein.

"These tulips are beautiful, Joey, I'll put them right in water. Becky will be out soon, she's almost ready."

So far so good. Nervously I looked around the apartment. It was nicely decorated. Modern. Lots of bookshelves filled with books. Real artwork on the walls. No Pope or Joe D. pictures in this house. I felt like a stranger in a strange land.

Mrs. Fishbein was very gracious. Welcoming even. She prepared a couple of cheese blintzes to eat in the movie. But Mr. Fishbein was more, shall I say, a challenge. The fact is he made me downright nervous asking me question after question, a Jewish Inquisition.

"Joseph, have you chosen a college yet?" he asked.

"Uh, well not yet," I answered.

"Well you better choose soon, time is of the essence," he warned.

"Yes, I will. Soon. I'm keeping my options open."

"Options are good, but there comes a time one has to act," he added.

"Leave him alone, Si. He's not even sixteen yet."

That's right, I thought. I'm not even sixteen. But stupid me I had to open my mouth.

"Actually, I'll be sixteen very soon," I offered.

"See, Isabel, before you know it, he'll be in high school. He has to prepare for his future."

Thank God Becky came out from the bathroom.

"Let's go," she said as she led me to the door.

"Don't stay out too late, sweetie, you have a chemistry test on Monday," Becky's father said.

"I have all day to study on Sunday, Dad. Bye."

And we were out the door. On the way to the theater she apologized for her father.

"He can get a little obnoxious at times, but he means well."

I assured her it was okay. My family could get obnoxious sometimes, too. Not that her father was obnoxious. It's all fine. All good. Not to worry.

We arrived at the movies. When we got to the ticket booth, I presented a dollar.

"Two, please," I said.

She put her hand on mine.

"I only go Dutch," she said.

"Dutch?" I asked.

"You know where the girl pays for herself. It's derived from a Dutch door where the two doors are equal. You've heard of a Dutch door?" Becky asked.

"Of course," I said, "my family is in construction, I know what a Dutch door is."

I had no idea what a Dutch door was. But I was very impressed that Becky knew. So, Becky went Dutch.

I was so nervous sitting next to Becky I hardly looked at the screen. I wanted to put my arm around her in the worst way but thought it might be too bold. After all it was our first date. I sat there frozen. For one and a half hours. A human icicle.

After the movie I invited her to go for a soda.

"Would you like to go for an egg cream?"

"Sure," she said. "As long as we.."

"..go Dutch, I know," finishing the sentence for her.

We went to Jack and Irv's, a few stores down from the theater. The local soda shop. These guys genuinely liked kids. Irv especially. He was always happy to see me. Actually, he was happy to see everybody. A gift, he had. He stood out in Brooklyn. An example of a truly happy person.

"Hey Joey, haven't seen you in a while. How's your father? I heard he just got back from Vietnam."

I didn't want to get into it, so I fibbed.

"He's doing good, Irv. Very good."

Then I tried to change the subject.

"You know Becky?" I asked.

"Of course, I know Becky, everybody knows Becky."

He looked at us.

"This wouldn't be a date, would it?" he asked.

"Yup," I said.

"We're going Dutch," Becky added, ever the feminist.

"Not in my store. Two free egg creams coming up."

"Thank you, Mr. Shatz," Becky said.

"So polite. I'm going to give you each a cherry."

I downed my egg cream in one gulp. Becky just sat there sipping her drink and smiling. I walked Becky home. I stopped at the entrance to the building. It was awkward. A handshake? A kiss on the cheek? The lips? I knew one thing I had to get out of there. I had to go pee from the egg cream. I gave her a peck on the cheek and raced home. My feet not touching the pavement. I was in love. No doubt about it. Head over heels in love. I raced up the stairs, ran into my bathroom. Slammed open the door, smashed the sink, and I went pee.

Becky and I began to hang out. Becky's father would have preferred she dated a Jewish boy, like Howie, well not like Howie, Howie. Even though we were just kids he didn't want to take any chances of her marrying a goy. So, we had to sneak around. Becky was welcome at my house, but I didn't dare go over there. Too bad it would have been a good place to hang. Both her parents worked. Her father was a college history teacher, her mom a paralegal. The house was empty all day.

My grandfather didn't think much of women working outside the home, but he made an exception for my mom since he and my grandmother enjoyed raising me, but he wasn't so kind to Becky's mom.

"She works all day, that's no way to raise a child."

He felt sorry for Becky, so he was okay with our relationship. 'Relationship' might be too fancy a word for what we had. We 'made out,' I got to first base as they said in the neighborhood. But Becky was a 'good girl'. In Brooklyn there were two types of girls. Good girls and whores. Or in Brooklynese 'who-as.' Good girls waited until they were married to 'do it' and who-as, well they 'did it' all the time. Becky was a good girl. So, we kept our activities safe.

We were a threesome, me, Howie, and Becky. Safety in numbers, isn't that what they say. Usually when the three of us were together we talked about our futures. Howie and Becky's career choices were pretty set. Howie was going to be a doctor, of course. You don't have Samuel Schwartz as your father and become a ditch digger. No offense to ditch diggers. Becky wanted to be a psychologist. I wished I had their certainty, but for me I'd have to try on a career for a while. Run it up the flagpole, see if it stuck.

"When I grow up, I want to be a writer," I declared.

"A writer, now?" Howie exclaimed. "You always do this. You watch 'What's My Line' on Sunday and then you choose a new career on Monday."

"No, I don't. I just think it's a good career. No heavy lifting, you can write at home. You don't have to go to an office. And people pay you a lot of money. My Aunt Theresa says I have the talent for it," I said.

"No offense to your Aunt Theresa but she doesn't get things right sometimes," Howie said.

"You do what you want to do, not what somebody tells you what you can or cannot do," Becky, the future shrink, said. That was one of the reasons I liked Becky, she was smart. Book smart. I often wondered what it would be like to carry a backpack full of books. School books. The only books we Italian boys might carry were Chilton Auto Repair manuals. Or maybe a how-to book. How to build a bookcase. A treehouse.

"Who's your favorite writer?" I asked Becky.

"I'd have to say Gertrude Goldberg."

"Who?" I asked.

"Gertrude Goldberg, she's a writer and comedienne. She has her own TV show."

"Plus, she's Jewish," Howie teased.

"I gotta go with Mario Puzo," I said.

"Who?" they asked in unison.

"He wrote "The Godfather." It's a best seller."

"Oh, I never heard of him," said Becky, "but if you say he's good, I'm sure he's good."

"Well I haven't actually read the book yet but Mrs. Scalise raves about it," I said.

"You know, you'd be a great writer," Becky said, smiling as she caressed my cheek. "Your birthday cards to me are soo romantic."

On that lovely note we arrived at school. I veered off to class 9-14 and Howie and Becky headed for class 9-1.

The one thing Italians were good at was shop. Woodworking and electrical, our favorites. The Jewish kids took leather shop. Mr. Blum gave them what he thought they could handle, braiding a lanyard to carry their keys or making a leather book cover. My woodworking teacher was Mr. Weinstein, 'Old Mahogany Head.' He was a Jewish guy teaching a bunch of Italian kids. It didn't compute. My electric shop teacher was Mr. Foy.

"Boys never urinate on the third rail," he'd say at the beginning of each term. "The urine will act as a conductor and you could get electrocuted."

Nice image, don't you think? It seemed a crazy thing to say, but Italian boys could do crazy things to prove their manhood.

On the way to my 9-14 homeroom class Charlie Giambo, and a few of his cronies, caught up with me. Charlie was a big bully who had given me trouble before. He didn't like the fact I hung out with Jewish kids. He considered me a traitor. Charlie's father and my grandfather did business together.

"Hey, Joey, heard your father's back from Nam," Charlie said in a whiny voice.

"Yeah, so," I said.

"So, my father says we're losing to the Commies. That makes your father a loser."

"Get lost, Charlie," I said dismissively.

"What'd you say?"

"You heard me," I said.

Charlie grabbed my lunch bag. He and his boys started to play 'Monkey in the Middle' and I was the monkey.

"Hey, my grandmother made me meatball sandwiches," I shouted.

My culinary appeal didn't work. Luckily Mr. Hunt came by. He was the Dean. He did yard duty and I had him for math.

"Charles, give Joseph back his lunch bag," he said.

Charlie gave the bag back to me slowly, making me reach for it.

"We were just playing, Mr. Hunt," Charlie fibbed.

Mr. Hunt looked to me for the truth. But the problem was the worst thing you could do in the neighborhood was rat on someone.

"Yeah, Mr. Hunt we were just playing," I mumbled.

"Well get to school now. Charles, I'm watching you."

Charlie went off and when he was out of Mr. Hunt's vision, he made threatening gestures at me like he was going to break my legs and arms. What a no count he was. God broke the mold when He made Charlie Giambo. And He broke it on purpose.

Mr. Hunt walked me to class.

"You know, Joseph, you shouldn't hang around people like Charles. You have the ability to go to college. You have a 129 IQ and you rarely get less than a hundred on your math tests. Plus, I spoke with your

English teacher, Mrs. Scalise and she said you are a gifted writer."

I thought, what's he doing talking to Mrs. Scalise? Maybe they ran out of things to talk about in the teachers' lounge and my name came up. It made me uncomfortable even though she always said nice things about me.

I walked into Mrs. Scalise's class and took my seat. The kids were horsing around, chasing each other. And I thought about what Mr. Hunt said as a spitball zinged past my ear and into the ear of Frankie Sissini, the boy sitting behind me.

College? Me? Joey Palumbo? He was kidding, right? What's all this talk about college. First Becky's dad, now Mr. Hunt. No one in my family had gone to college. Or even thought about going to college. It seemed far-fetched. A distant dream. A wish. A song. Wait, correction. My cousin, Rosemary went to college, St. Joseph's College in the Clinton Hill section of Brooklyn. Might as well have been on the moon as far as the family was concerned. Her mother, Aunt Nettie encouraged her to go.

"It'll be good for her, 'broaden her horizons'."

My aunt lived around the block on 20th avenue. She was a lay teacher at a Catholic school or as they called it in Brooklynese, Catlick school. Mrs. 'G' the kids called her. Her husband's last name was Gugliotta. Uncle Leo died a few years ago. He was the barber in the family. After he passed, I went to Joe Passalaqua on 71st street and then Roberto Bonagura, Bob for short, on 72nd street. Bob, who just got off the boat, was a sweetheart. You'd sit in his barber chair and he'd ask in broken English how you wanted it cut. I'd say: "Crewcut." And he'd say every time: "You the boss, me the horse." And then he did whatever he wanted.

I would help my aunt grade her students' composition tests. She saw a bright future for me. She single-handedly was trying to upgrade the intellectual achievement of the Palumbo family. At best an uphill battle.

After college my aunt and cousin moved to Long Island. Way the heck out. Almost the last stop on the Long Island Railroad. Smithtown. As far away from Brooklyn as they could get. My aunt died a year later from a heart attack. My grandfather said she died of a broken heart, she missed Brooklyn so much. Who knows? My grandfather thought college was the beginning of the end of family. And he would always point to Rosemary as proof.

"She's away from her family, what kind of life is that?" he said.

"She's a real estate broker. She has her own company," my mother would invariably point out.

"Big deal, her own company. She's away from her family, what kind of life is that?" he'd repeat.

I knew enough to keep secret any talk of college from my grandfather.

Mrs. Scalise walked into the room. The kids quieted down. Mrs. Scalise was tough but inspirational. She gave the class her yearly pep talk:

"This year I want you to aim higher than you ever thought possible. You are the descendants of great writers, like Dante, Boccaccio, Machiavelli.."

Just then an eraser was hurled off the blackboard. The class cracked up. Mrs. Scalise turned to Sal Glorioso, the class clown.

"Salvatore, after school you will write on the blackboard 500 times, I won't throw erasers in class."

"Does that mean I can throw them when I'm not in class?" Again, the class cracked up.

I looked around the room at the kids laughing and began to wonder. "Dante, Boccaccio, Machiavelli? What happened to us? How'd we slip so far?" Then Mrs. Scalise restored order:

"Class, for your term paper this year I want you to write about a problem someone close to you is having. Writers are problem solvers. Brave souls who go into dark rooms looking for answers. Answers to things that are important to them. Things that scare them. Things that eat away at their souls."

On my way to my next class I thought about what I could write about. A problem someone close to me was having. Hmm. Then it hit me. My father was having a problem adjusting to civilian life and he was close to me. Bingo. This year's paper. Excited, I went to the school library and got some books on Vietnam. Research, the name of the game. That's one thing I learned from my grandmother. Do your work ahead of time. She'd make her sauce for Sunday dinner the night before. Then when Sunday came, bam, she just had to warm it up, add some seasonings. Made for stress free cooking. So that became my motto for everything:

"Make the sauce the night before."

During lunch I often went to my grandfather's business office and did my schoolwork. While I was walking through the yard that day, I noticed a big change around there. The yard was full of large equipment. Backhoes, cranes, dump trucks sitting idle.

The men were sitting around having lunch, taking a break from various make work jobs. Stacking lumber. Re-stacking lumber. Stacking it again. It was sad to see. These were talented men, carpenters, big equipment operators. I loved those guys. Black, Italian, Irish, a Puerto Rican. My grandfather didn't care. Only the work counted. You did good work, showed up on time and you could work for him.

My favorite was Ernie Simms. Ernie was the company's foreman. He'd been with the company for over twenty years. Started out as a laborer. He was so good at it that my grandfather let him hold the tape measure as he shot measurements with a transit for a foundation. Soon Ernie was the one looking through the transit eyehole and my grandfather was holding the tape. He went on from there to be an apprentice carpenter and then on up to be the foreman. In a different time, Ernie would have had his own company, but Ernie was black. That kept him tethered to the company. But Ernie didn't resent it. He respected my grandfather and thankful for giving him a chance for a good paying job and a good life.

Prior to Ernie my only contact with a black person was in grade school, P.S. 247, on 67th street, five blocks away from the house. His name was John Page. John hardly spoke. And when he did it came out as a whisper. Obviously being the only black person in a sea of white faces was intimidating. He retreated into a shell. They seated the kids alphabetically and I sat behind John. I never exchanged two words with him. His father was the janitor at The Le Parc so that's where he lived. I knew nothing else about him. Did he have a mother? I didn't know. Was he a good person? I didn't know. What was his favorite sport? I didn't know that either. I wanted to reach out to him. I thought about it all the time. But I didn't. Strangely enough that's one of my biggest regrets in life - not talking to John Page.

Ernie Simms was nothing like John except for the color of his skin. Ernie was outgoing, engaging. He wouldn't wait for you to approach him.

"Hey, Joe, when are we going to get us some of your Grandma's lasagna? Huh? You holding out on us?"

"Someday, Ernie, someday," I'd assure him.

"We're growing old waiting." All the men laughed. Once in a great while I would sit and have lunch with them. I was always amazed how smart they were and what they talked about. The stock market, politics, art. They were a lot smarter than people gave them credit for.

Ernie was also a tease. He used to fake punching me. "You flinched. That's two," he'd say.

He then punched me twice in the arm. Not hard but enough to keep me on my toes. That's another thing we did in Brooklyn, punch each other in the arm. Either when you made the other guy flinch or when you 'Got him.' Howie and I always tried to 'get' each other. My best 'get' with Howie was in his bedroom. We were looking out the window and I saw Larry Seltzer walking towards us. Larry was the neighborhood nebbish to be avoided at all cost. Howie didn't notice yet, so I waited until Larry was close to us and I yelled out the window, "Hey Seltzer." Then I ducked down on my hands and knees leaving Howie at the window alone. Mean, I know. Larry stopped.

"Hi Howie, wanna wrestle?"

"No thanks, Seltzer."

Larry shrugged and then left.

"Gotcha! That's two."

I hit Howie twice on the arm. For some reason kids don't do this anymore. But it was an awful lot of fun.

Anyway, I headed to the office loaded down with books on Vietnam. Not much work for the men meant not much work in the office for my Aunt Jenny. She was the company bookkeeper. She tried her best to stay busy. When I entered the office, I saw her at her desk with a black felt pen and she was circling something in a newspaper. When she saw me, she quickly ditched the newspaper, hiding it in a drawer. I took out my books and started to read about Vietnam, taking notes.

I realized that my family had a lot of secrets. I figured it was because we were so enmeshed in each other's lives that a secret gave you some breathing room. Some space. Some much needed space.

That next Sunday I did what I always did in the morning. I read the sports section of the Daily News. My father sat across from me, reading the rest of the paper. The Daily News didn't stir the intellect, but it had the best sports section. Post, Mirror, Daily News. Those were the newspapers Italian people read. If you wanted insight you read the Reader's Digest. Becky's parents read the Wall Street Journal. Howie's, the New

York Times. Now that was a paper. World events, national and local news, editorials, a business section. It was so big you had to fold it into sections to read it. I didn't know of one Italian who read the New York Times. Not one. If they did, they would be opening themselves up to ridicule.

"Who does he think he is reading the New York Times? He's putting on airs. What's he trying to prove? World events? National news? What's it his business?"

That's how we were programmed. Think only about your neighborhood, your block, your family. Think small. But I was writing a term paper and I had my subject right across from me, so I decided what the heck, I'd take a chance.

"Dad, do you think the war in Vietnam was worth it?" I asked hiding behind my newspaper.

"I don't know. Your country calls you to serve so you go," he said behind his newspaper. So far so good.

"Do you believe in the Domino theory? That if Vietnam goes to the Communists so will the rest of Asia?" I asked, still behind the paper.

"Yes, I do," my Dad said behind his paper.

I put the newspaper down and went for it.

"I read where a lot of soldiers are coming home agitated, having trouble adjusting to civilian life."

My father put his newspaper down.

"What's all the questions on Vietnam?

"Mrs. Scalise asked us to do a term paper on a problem someone close to us is having. I figured, you know, I could do it about you. If that's okay?"

My father didn't answer. I tried to sell the idea.

"She said writers are problem solvers. Brave souls who go in dark rooms looking for answers. Answers to things that are important to them. Things that scare them. Things that eat away at their souls," I repeated her words.

"Choose another person," he said.

Just what I thought. My father didn't want to talk about the war. This term paper was going to be harder to write than I thought. I decided not to push. Besides I had something else on my mind. I put down my paper.

"Dad, how come nobody in our family went to college?" I asked.

"That's not true. Your cousin, Rosemary went to college."

"I mean us males."

"I don't know. Just not something we aspire to."

"Mrs. Scalise thinks I'm college material. She said I have a gift for writing. That I'm a descendent of Dante, Boccaccio, Machiavelli, and Gioannino Guareschi.

"Who?" my father asked.

"Gioannino Guareschi. Mrs. Scalise gave me a copy of his short stories – the *Little World of Don Camillo*, an Italian priest," I said.

"Mrs. Scalise has taken a real interest in you," my father noticed.

"You'd like her, Dad. She was in the Army. If someone makes some lame excuse for not doing their homework she tells them how it was in the Army. If your superior asked you why you did something wrong you'd shout out, "NO EXCUSE, SIR!" I want to tell her it may have worked in the Army but it's not going to work in Class 9-14. Not with cutups Jimmy Passentino and Freddy Grasso in the class."

We shared a laugh.

"Mr. Hunt, the Dean, also thinks I'm college material. They talk about me to each other," I said.

"Oh? Why does he say that?"

"My IQ is high, and I do very well on English and Math standardized tests. Like the Jewish kids."

"You can go to college if you want," he said.

"If I went to college what would I study? I wish I was more certain of my future like Howie and Becky."

My father moved his chair right next to mine, his face two inches away. That's what paisanos do when they want to make a point. They don't want *air* to get in the way.

"Son, don't ever compare yourself to anyone. They may seem better off than you but you never really know about their lives unless you walk in their shoes. Be your own person. That's all that matters."

I thought my father was a very smart man. He could've gone to college. Maybe he could have been an engineer. Hey, maybe I could go to college for the both of us. Anyway, before I had a chance to continue our discussion of college my mother came in waving what looked to be a check. It was a check. Her first commission in 'the real estate.'

"My deal closed!" she exclaimed.

"Hey, congratulations!" my father said.

"Yeah, Ma, congratulations."

"We should go out today, just the three of us. Celebrate," my mother said.

"Hey, how about the new Chinese Restaurant on Bay Parkway? The New Deal. Becky's family goes there every Sunday. She says it's great," I suggested, getting in the festive mood.

"Great," my father said, "I don't think I can stand another dinner talking about construction and how things will pick up now that I'm back."

"Amen to that," my mother chimed in.

We put on our coats and hats and started to rush out the door, practically giddy, when we heard thumping from the floor below. My grandmother was signaling us with her broom. Time for Sunday dinner. Oh, well, maybe another time.

My grandfather was dominating the conversation..

"Things will pick up now that Danny's back. You're good with people, Danny. I get impatient sometimes. I never should've given up working with my tools. I'm better working, not holding clipboards and pointing," my grandfather said.

My father was squirming in his seat, I had to do something. Say something.

"I have an idea. Let's not talk about construction today. Let's talk about something else... Something worldly. Something in the newspaper. Becky showed me this article in the New York Times about Vietnam and whether we should get out," I said.

"Huh?" "Vietnam?" "What are you crazy?"

My father excused himself saying he had to do an estimate for a possible job. He left the table. My mother's eyes followed him out. She knew he wasn't right. I had heard them whispering in the bedroom. I heard her say he should 'see someone.' A therapist. But that is the last avenue Italian men wanted to pursue. You solved your own problems. Alone. Like a man.

"Let's talk about something else," my mother said.

Choruses of "Yeah." "Something else." 'Something lighter."

My grandfather excused himself to go to the bathroom. He did that a lot. It's "the age," he'd say.

"Okay, okay, something else," I said, "something lighter." All agreed that was the way to go.

"Who wants to go first? Grandma how about you? Tell us about your day," I said.

"Ask somebody else," she said.

"No, Grandma, I'm asking you. Tell us about your day."

My grandmother thought hard trying to remember what she did.

"Well, I cooked breakfast. Cleaned the house. Then I made dinner for everybody," she recounted. Then she stopped talking.

"That's it?" I asked.

"That's it," she said. "Oh, I also saw Flamenco dancers on the television. I made a promise to myself. One day I'm going to Spain to see them in person."

Everyone agreed she should make that happen. I looked around the table. Everyone shrank in their chairs not wanting to be called on.

"Ma. You had some news today," I said.

"I closed my first deal," my mother offered modestly. Cheers erupted around the table.

"I knew it. She has the head," Aunt Theresa professed.

"She definitely has the head," Aunt Jenny joked. (ala Groucho Marx) "And the rest of her ain't too bad either."

Everyone laughed.

"Aunt Jenny, how about you? What'd you do today?" I asked.

Aunt Jenny looked at the bathroom door to make sure my grandfather couldn't hear.

"Well, I've been reading the personals in the newspaper," Aunt Jenny revealed.

"What's that?" Uncle Tommy asked.

"You know, man seeking woman, woman seeking man. What a matchmaker did in the old days. Only now you do it yourself."

"That's wonderful, Jenny. Women in my office have had a lot of success finding a mate that way," my mother said, offering encouragement.

"I don't know, lots of perverts out there. Sounds risky," Uncle Tommy said worried about his sister.

"Maybe. But I'm at the stage where I have to take some risks. In case you haven't noticed I haven't exactly been the belle of the ball," Aunt Jenny said half joking.

"She's looking for a prince. For a princess," my grandmother lovingly offered.

"From your lips to God's ear," said Aunt Jenny.

"That's just great, Aunt Jenny, just great," I chimed in.

"But let's not mention it to you know who," Aunt Jenny whispered.

Everyone knew who she was talking about.

"Mention what? What did I miss?" my grandfather asked as he returned from the bathroom.

After what seemed like an eternity I managed to eke out, "I've been meaning to tell you, Grandpa I'm *thinking* about becoming a writer. Just thinking."

"I can't believe what I'm hearing. Am I the only one who doesn't know this?" he wondered as he looked around the table.

Nobody said a word. Uncle Frankie jumped in.

"Who knows, maybe he'd be good at it," he said.

My grandfather handed down the proclamation.

"This is a family of builders!" he declared.

Everyone went back to eating. Only the clanging of utensils on plates could be heard the rest of the dinner.

Chapter 3
Creditors Come Calling

Seth Low Park

After school I usually stopped by Seth Low Park to shoot around. I was called 'The Mayor' of Seth Low Park. I had other nicknames. 'Pope,' 'Commissioner,' but 'The Mayor' was my favorite. It had a nice ring to it. I put in a lot of time taking care of the courts. If it snowed, I'd bring a shovel to clear it off. If it rained, I'd bring a mop. Leaves? No problem got a broom right here. I couldn't bear not to play. It would have constituted cruel and unusual punishment from the basketball Gods. There were 2 full courts. 4 baskets. The 'A' court is where the Lafayette High School varsity basketball team played. They could really play. Mostly

European and Syrian Jews. The Italians played baseball. I played both but for some reason basketball was my passion. I couldn't wait to play on the 'A' court, but I just wasn't old enough, not strong enough. Still I played as if my life depended on it. Yup, it was life and death in Seth Low Park. The mecca for Bensonhurst basketball.

Sometimes I shot around alone on the 'B' court. I did my own play by play. I banked one off the backboard. "Bank's open," I'd say. Then I'd launch a hook shot from ten feet. "Houbregs," I called out. Bob Houbregs played for the Fort Wayne Pistons. It was before my time, but he had a dead accurate hook shot from ten to twelve feet which I adopted because I was short and had trouble shooting over taller defenders. Plus, I liked how it sounded, 'Houbregs!' I was a rabid Knicks fan so I couldn't leave out Dick Barnett. Barnett used to kick his legs up behind him as he shot his jump shot. Unorthodox and deadly. I could imitate his herk jerky motion to a tee.

"Barnett from the key. Swish. Barnett off the glass. Count it.

I also pretended I played for the Knicks.

"Knicks down by one against the dreaded Boston Celtics, ten seconds left on the clock, Palumbo dribbles the ball at the top of the key, Havlicek guarding him, five seconds left, he shakes, he bakes, one second, he shoots. Good!! The Knicks win the N.B.A. Championship! Yay!!!"

After ball I often stopped by the business office. Through the window I could see a big commotion was going on in the yard. My grandfather was standing in front of a huge backhoe blocking it from being driven off our property. Jimmy Giambo, Charlie's father, was repossessing a piece of equipment for non-payment of his bill.

"I'm not moving," my grandfather fumed defiantly.

"I can't carry you anymore, Vince," Jimmy said.

"Carry me? Nobody carries me. I carry you," my grandfather said.

Jimmy motioned to his guy to drive forward. The goon revved up the motor trying his best to scare my grandfather. The problem was my grandfather didn't scare. Even if he did, he wasn't going to give in. He was one of those men if you fought him, you'd have to kill him. I had to do something. A moveable object was about to meet an immoveable force.

I dashed outside as fast as I could. I began pulling at my grandfather's arm. He wouldn't budge. More revving, more pulling, revving, pulling. A standoff.

Suddenly my father drove up in his pick-up truck. He had been in Staten Island looking at property. Now my father didn't get angry, but that was then, before his Army days. But he was angry now.

"What's going on?" my father demanded to know.

"We haven't received a payment on the backhoe in three months, Danny," Jimmy explained.

"You'll get your money. Your father never lost one cent because of me," my grandfather said.

"I have bills to pay. If Palumbo & Sons can't pay for this machine, I have to find someone who can."

"This is crazy. We can work something out," my father fumed.

"I wish I could, Dan. Now move Vince."

My grandfather gently led me out of the way, rolled up his sleeves and with absolute defiance declared:

"You're gonna have to run me over."

Giambo was equally angry, he motioned to his guy. The goon revved up the motor. My grandfather stood there daring him to run him over. Suddenly, my father jumped on the backhoe. In one swift motion he grabbed the keys to the ignition and tossed them away.

"Now, nobody's doing anything!" he declared.

You had to be there. Giambo's face dropped. To his toes. He underestimated the loyalty of the Palumbos. When attacked we circle the wagons.

"I can call the cops, Danny. I'm in my rights."

My father jumped down, got in Giambo's face. Yup, two inches away.

"Don't you ever come here again and talk to my father like that. You'll get your money. Now get the hell off our property!"

Whoa, the war had certainly changed my father. It was as if he had something bubbling inside that could boil over at any time. Giambo looked at my father, then my grandfather and then for some reason he looked at me. I didn't know why he looked at me, maybe he was hoping I could talk some sense into these two angry men. But I was not about to even try. If I was going to be a writer, now was the time to apply my trade.

"Yeah," I said, the only word I could think of.

Jimmy thought for a few moments and decided discretion was the better part of valor. He motioned to his goon to follow him out.

"One month. That's it." They left.

One month? Even I knew that wasn't much time. I also knew a backhoe was the most important piece of equipment a construction company could have. You needed it to dig a trench for a foundation. No foundation, no house. The three of us went inside the main office and my grandfather had his arm around each of us.

"We showed him, boys. We showed him."

"Yeah, Pop, we showed him," my father said looking down at the ground.

Then the two men went into my grandfather's office to talk. I listened at the door. My father started off the conversation.

"Okay, we made it through today, but what're we going to do next month. How're we going to come up with the money?"

"We'll think of something," my grandfather said.

"What, Pop? What?" my father asked earnestly.

"I don't know yet," my grandfather responded.

Then it got quiet for a while.

"We might have to let some of the men go," my father reluctantly said.

"No!" my grandfather said, sternly.

"We have the Grosso job but nothing after that," my father said, trying to make his case.

"I don't care. These men have worked for us their whole lives, we can't just throw them out in the street," my grandfather said.

"Pop, maybe we should think about declaring bankruptcy."

Had my father forgotten who he was talking to? My grandfather reminded him.

"Declare bankruptcy??? I'd rather shoot myself," he said.

"Well, maybe you can come up with another idea, because I'm out of ideas!" my father fumed, losing patience.

Then I heard my grandfather talk, in a calm voice, confident. The kind of confidence that comes when you are good at what you do. And you've done it for a long time.

"There are plenty of ideas. All we have to do is think."

That was it, end of discussion.

They started to come out and I quickly grabbed my notebook and took off to school. I ran the whole way. Fast. Jesse Owens fast. My heart was racing. I began to sweat. The ground was spinning. I was feeling sick. I needed to throw up.

I made it to the toilet in the boys' bathroom. Well, the sink actually. Mr. Hunt happened to come in and saw me. He said if I was sick, he could write a note to send me home. I didn't want to tell him home was the problem. The great thing about Mr. Hunt was he knew when to give you space. Obviously not a Brooklyn native. He was from Vermont. He came to Brooklyn because his wife wanted to come back home and take care of her mother. He washed his hands and exited, leaving me to clean up. My world was suddenly turned upside down. I'd heard of the phrase "declaring bankruptcy" before. I knew it wasn't just going on the roof of The Le Parc and shouting at the top of your lungs, "People, as of this moment I am out of money."

I knew it involved accountants and attorneys and caused great emotional pain to all those involved. I knew this because it happened to someone in the family. Uncle Paul.

Uncle Paul was married to Aunt Fran, my mother's sister. They lived on 38th street. Aunt Fran was sweet, we called her "Dear Dear," But she was a little potz. Actually, a lot potz. To give you an idea, they lived on the second floor of Uncle Pat's apartment building. Aunt Fran was cleaning the outside of her windows standing on the ledge. Then she stepped back to admire her work and fell to the pavement breaking both her ankles. The crazy thing was she told the truth about what happened. She could have made something up, there were no video cameras then.

One more thing and you'll have a good picture of her. If there was a new baby in the family, Aunt Fran would stand behind the baby and clap her hands. Three times. Loud. If the baby didn't move, she was declared deaf. If she reacted, Aunt Fran would give her the Aunt Fran hearing seal of approval.

"No problem with this baby, she can hear," she certified.

As you can imagine Uncle Paul had his hands full with her. As far as gainful employment he was it. He was always concocting some get rich scheme. Some ideas weren't bad. In fact, he included me in one. We went around to used car lots and spray-painted headliners. I masked the car off first, Uncle Paul sprayed afterwards. He paid me $8 an hour. Good money for that time. His plan was to go big, train people to do the spraying while he stayed home and waited for the money to roll in. The problem was he needed investors to buy the equipment and nobody would give him money because they were burned by previous failed deals. But Uncle Paul kept on trying. Looking for that one irresistible idea. One day he came up with it. He would sell trophies to deer hunters. Yup, shoot a deer, you buy a trophy for yourself.

"Genius," Aunt Fran said, "my husband's a genius."

That should have been a clue right there, but Uncle Paul went ahead anyway. Uncle Sal loaned him a good chunk of the money. Some investors followed, figuring if he didn't pay, Uncle Sal would have his legs broken. Uncle Sal felt by loaning money to family it somehow made his illegal activities okay. Or at least less crooked. Anyway, with his newfound capital Uncle Paul had all the deer trophies made. He got a storefront and waited for the deer hunters to come bounding in. Problem was it was more of a trickle than a bound. He was forced to declare bankruptcy. For the last time.

Uncle Sal felt sorry for him, so he let him go. But a year after that Uncle Paul was so distraught, he ran away, never to be seen again. I got to know Uncle Paul as we drove to the car lots. It wasn't only about the money, Uncle Paul wanted to be somebody. Not the worst thing in the world. He just couldn't get there.

But this was different, right? This wasn't Uncle Paul, this was Palumbo & Sons, the best builders in Brooklyn! That night I couldn't sleep. I was worried my grandfather would do the unthinkable. Take off for points unknown. I loved my grandfather. I couldn't imagine a world without him. But what was I going to do? I couldn't give him money; I didn't have any. I felt powerless. The only solace I had was my father couldn't sleep that night either. Then out of the dark of night I heard these words from behind my parents' cracked bedroom door:

"Gina, I want you to do something for me," my father said.

"Sure, Danny. What?" She asked.

"I want you to do a comparative market analysis. I think we should think about closing down the business and selling the property," he said.

Then the door closed. This didn't happen a lot. Only when they were making love or when they wanted me not to 'accidentally' hear them. There wasn't much love making since my father returned from the war so that couldn't be it. It must have been the latter. But I had heard enough. That property had been in my family for fifty years. I didn't like what I was hearing. I had to tell somebody. I wondered if Becky might be up at eleven in the night. She saw things clearly. She could put it all in perspective.

I got dressed quickly and sneaked out of the apartment and ran up 72nd street to her building. I knew Becky's ground-floor bedroom window fronted the street so I tossed some pebbles at it hoping she would hear me. She didn't. I jumped over the short metal guard rail and went to her window and tapped on it. Tap, tap, tap. Nothing. I listened carefully. Then I scrunched my face on the window and peered in. A lamp was on by the bed and I could see Becky was lying in bed reading. I tapped again. Louder.

"Becky, it's me," I whispered.

Becky quickly got out of bed and opened the window. I climbed in. Becky quickly closed her bedroom door so her parents wouldn't be disturbed.

Then she turned on the overhead light. I sat at the foot of her bed, she at the top by the pillows. Like most girls she could tuck her legs under her torso. I had to dangle mine over the bed.

"What are you doing here? My father would plotz if he knew," she said.

Plotz. What a great Yiddish word. It meant burst. There were three distinct foreign languages spoken in the neighborhood by the older generation. Italian, Arabic and Yiddish. Such a colorful language, Yiddish. I often wondered why Brooklyn didn't adopt it as its official language. I would have voted for it. Plotz, for burst, chutzpah meaning having guts, shvitz for sweat. The words sounded like their meaning.

I told her what had happened at the yard and the possible ramifications for my family. But as I spoke the surroundings caught my eye. I couldn't believe a kid my age lived like this. A state-of-the-art stereo system with four Bose speakers hung high up in the four corners of the room. The bed was the canopy type. Made of cherry wood. The mattress was a Duxiana, the brand used on Park Avenue, in Manhattan. But the most amazing thing about the room, were the books. There were books everywhere. In bookcases, on the desk, on nightstands, on the bed, under the bed. I had to ask.

"You read all these?"

"Most of them," she said.

"Wow. I've always wondered what it was like to carry a bunch of books in a backpack. But the kids in my class would make fun of me."

"Books are the window to the soul," she said.

"That's good, I'll have to remember that."

This was the first time I had been in Becky's bedroom or more importantly seen Becky in pajamas. They were yellow with tiny red hearts all over them. Adorable.

"I have no idea what to tell you," she said. "We're not risk takers in my family. We work for other people. I have no point of reference," she said.

"Oh," I said, disappointed.

"I don't know a thing about declaring bankruptcy or selling property. The only assets in my family are cash, stocks and Treasury bonds," she said.

"You must have some people in your family, uncles, cousins, whatever who are in business for themselves."

"Actually, I do have one. My Uncle Sid. He sells pants. You know, Sid's Pants on Kings Highway?"

"That's your uncle? The guy with the psoriasis?"

"That's him."

"So, what does he do when business is bad? He must do something."

"He advertises."

"He advertises. Of course," I said, relieved.

"I think you better go now. It's late. I have temple tomorrow."

I left. Like I came in, through the window. I ran home. Advertise, that's it! Coke does it, Ford Motors does it.

As I climbed the stairs to my apartment, slogans began flooding into my head. 'Have us redo your kitchen and we'll throw in a bathroom.' Or 'We do God's work. So, recommend us. Palumbo & Sons, the Godly choice.' Not bad I thought. At least as good as the Castro Convertible Sofa commercial. Then as I snuck back into my apartment and into my open bed, I realized something. Advertising costs money and that's what we didn't have. We were sunk!!

That next morning my parents were at the seldom used dining room table going over a bunch of numbers. I pretended to be still asleep. My mother had gotten the comps my father asked for. Similar property in the neighborhood was going for two hundred thousand, two fifty even. My father couldn't believe how much things had changed while he was gone. My mother told him about a Chinese agent who represented a group in Taiwan who was looking to put up apartment houses. And that sometimes they paid more than market.

"How come?" my father asked.

"They come here with money handed down from generation to generation, these prices seem cheap. Want to meet him?" my mother asked.

"You're the agent," my father reminded her.

"Oh no. If I made a commission on the family your father would kill me," she said. "Here's his card. You call him."

My father stared at that card for the longest time. He did that a lot now. Stare at things. As if he needed to focus on it to really understand it. Then he tucked the card into his shirt pocket.

My mother went to work. I pretended to just wake up and my father grabbed the papers and put them in a folder. He didn't want me to see them. The less I knew the better. After all I was only fifteen.

A week passed. Things weren't getting better at the company and time was running out. One day after school I was working in the backyard with my grandfather. We were putting up the grape arbor my grandfather had been working on. I liked working with him. I was learning from the master. Everything was precut and fit perfectly. Like a jigsaw puzzle.

My grandmother was out there as well, tending the tomatoes she used for her macaroni sauce. My father and Uncle Tommy came up to them, their bodies blocking the sun as it peeked out from oncoming dark clouds. My mother lagged behind them a few steps.

"Hey Pop, we want to talk to you about something," my father said.

Well that usually meant without me so I gracefully tried to excuse myself. I had a term paper to do.

"Stay, Joey, this concerns you, too," my father said.

Whoa, that's a first. I was being included.

We all sat down at a glass top outdoor table. It had an umbrella in the center to help block the sun's rays. It was strange sitting together with no food involved. In fact, I couldn't remember this happening before.

"Anybody want some cold cuts?" my grandmother finally asked.

Nope, not today. Uncle Tommy nudged my father. You talk first.

"Pop, we've been thinking. About our futures. About all our futures. Anyway, Tommy's thinking maybe he'd like to open a gym. In Florida. Tell him, Tom."

"Yeah, Pop. I know about gyms. I've spent my whole life in them. I think I can make a go of it. I'd have the latest gym equipment. Good stuff, that works. Not like the junk at Vito's. It'd be first class. No plastic, only leather. I'd have these showers, with massage units in the shower heads. And beautiful lockers. Red. I gotta have red lockers. And carpeting, thick..."

Uncle Tommy stopped in mid-sentence. He knew he was losing his audience. My grandfather looked at my grandmother as if to say where is this coming from?

Then it was my father's turn.

"And Gina and I are thinking maybe we'd like to relocate to Staten Island, they have nice homes there, reasonable, too. Gina's company has an office there, I'd work for Uncle Sal at first then go out on my own."

Whoa, relocate to Staten Island? I could barely control myself. And forget about my grandfather, Mt. Vesuvius was about to blow. My grandmother put her hand on his. "Aspetti." Wait.

My father went on with his spiel.

"So, we were thinking, now that business is down, maybe it's a good time to close up shop and sell the property."

He breathed a sigh of relief. He got it out.

I looked at my grandfather, waited for his reaction.

"Sell the property?" he could hardly get the words out.

My father quickly asked my mother to show him the numbers. She placed a sheet of paper on the table in front of Vince.

"Recent sales in the neighborhood." Not wanting my grandfather to think it was her idea she quickly added, "Danny asked me to compile it."

My grandfather glanced at the list. My grandmother looked over his shoulder.

"Plus, Gina gave me the name of this Chinese agent, Mr. Lee, who has clients who might even be willing to pay more. I just have to call him," my father added.

I looked up at the dark clouds overhead hoping they would bring forth the promised deluge and stop this. It didn't help to bring a Chinese person in the mix. My grandfather was not happy about the Chinese coming into Bensonhurst and buying up property.

"So, what do you think, Pop?" my father asked.

"Yeah, Pop, what do you think?" Uncle Tommy mimicked.

My grandfather looked down at the list. The eruption was near, I'd soon have molten lava all over me.

"We're in a slump and this is what you do? You meet behind my back and discuss things our family put their whole lives into. And this is how you repay them?"

"Pop don't do this. We're doing it for you, too. You won't have to work anymore. You and Ma can go on that vacation to Spain she's always talking about."

"I like that part." My grandmother cut in trying to diffuse the situation.

"Or just sit back and rest. Live off the interest with your share," my father added.

"My share?? My share?? I didn't work my whole life with these (displaying the nuclear deterrents) hands to sit around and live off the interest with my share!! You want to know what I think? This is what I think!!"

He took that paper in his hands and tore it up violently. Then stormed off. My father was crushed, it went a lot worse than he had feared. My grandmother put a comforting hand on his shoulder: "I'll talk to him." My grandmother followed my grandfather inside.

These were hopeful words. Not used often. But if anyone could get my grandfather to reconsider it was my grandmother. Such was the power of his love and her food.

Suddenly the rain began to pour down and we ran for cover. It came a little too late. We decided to try that Chinese restaurant, the New Deal. I had mixed feelings. I was unhappy I wasn't included in the discussion to move to Staten Island but at least I was included after the fact. I was feeling pretty good actually, in a strange way, empowered.

But the mood at the restaurant matched the weather. Gloomy. We looked at our menus. Since we rarely went to a Chinese restaurant, in fact we never went to a Chinese restaurant, the menu presented quite a challenge. Crab Rangoon, Kung Pao shrimp, Moo goo gai pan, Szechuan pork? I thought to myself, where's the spaghetti and meatballs? Can't you see we're Italian? God forbid we asked the waiter to explain any of the dishes. Oh no we should know how to order. The waiter returned to take our orders.

"Any questions?" he asked.

"No, we're good," my father said.

I decided to play it safe. Go with what Becky told me was good.

"I'll have the pork lo mein," I said.

"Me, too," my father said.

"Me, too," my mother said.

"Me, too," Uncle Tommy said.

We returned the menus quickly to the waiter before he had the nerve to question our selections. The waiter went off mumbling something to himself in Chinese. Then we sat there and waited for our food. The four of us sipping Chinese tea from tiny cups with blue flowers on them. I was worried about my uncle spilling the tea. My eyes were glued to his cup. But Uncle Tommy was doing surprisingly well. Oops spoke too soon, tea all over the table. The waiter quickly returned and just as quickly gave us a new tablecloth. As he was leaving, he took away Uncle Tommy's little cup. Smart people, the Chinese, I thought. We waited some more. My mother broke the silence.

"Joey, what do you think about us moving to Staten Island?"

"I don't know, Ma, I'd have to think about that. Becky is here, all my friends are here."

"But you can make new friends and we'd only be an hour away. I saw this great house. You could have your own bedroom, and a dog even, and there's grass both in the front and back yard."

Low blow, she knew I had a thing for grass. Maybe because there was so much concrete in Brooklyn.

"But Grandpa will never sell the business," I said, "so what's the use in talking about it."

Then my mother thought for a moment. You could almost see a lightbulb go off in her head.

"You know, Dan, you and Tommy can do this on your own," she said.

"What do you mean?" my father asked.

"Yeah, what do you mean?" asked Uncle Tommy.

"You each own a third of the business. You can outvote your father?" she advised.

"You're forgetting one thing, Ma," I said.

"What's that?" she asked.

"Grandpa's third is awfully big," I said.

One third is not always one third. You couldn't learn that in Mr. Hunt's math class. No sirree. You had to come to the New Deal.

The lo mein came and it was great. We congratulated each other on making such a wise choice. I didn't dare tell my grandmother though. She didn't like for us to eat on 'the outside.'

"You never know what they put into the food," she would always warn.

One time we did get food to go. My grandmother had the flu, so we were forced to bring something in. It was from an Indian restaurant. And when my father returned with the food there was a staple in the Tandoori chicken. Obviously having gotten there when they stapled the bag closed. That was it. Never again. Aunt Jenny would make the joke that next time they got Indian food, ask for the Tandoori chicken and tell them to hold the staples. A big laugh around the house, except my grandmother. She failed to see the humor and promised never to get sick again. So, we didn't tell her if we got takeout.

Another secret. I was beginning to lose track and began to wonder if Jewish families kept things from each other. I'd have to ask Howie the next time I saw him. Later that next day my grandmother told my father that her attempt to convince my grandfather to sell the property didn't work. He wouldn't budge. We were running out of time and options. But I always felt my grandfather would find a way. Superman always saved the day, right?

After that day in the backyard I began to hang around my grandfather more. The lines of loyalty were being drawn and I felt everyone was ganging up on him and he was now the underdog. I always rooted for the underdog. Everyone in Brooklyn rooted for the underdog. We knew in our hearts we were all underdogs in a world of overdogs. That's why most Brooklynites rooted for the Brooklyn Dodgers. 'Dem bums', as they were affectionately called.

That is one thing my grandfather and me shared. We were both rabid Dodger fans. My grandfather used to take me to games in Ebbetts Field. It was their final year in Brooklyn, 1957. I was only seven at the time, but I still remember my first glimpse of that infield. I'd walk up to the ticket taker, hand over my ticket, walk through the turnstile and then up a concrete walkway. Then I'd see it. Peeking out through the grandstands on either side, beautiful emerald green grass, with an incredibly groomed tan dirt infield. It took my breath away. Every time we went that year, same thing. Grass has been magical for me ever since.

I was sad to see the Dodgers go. I didn't understand the politics of it all, but I sensed it was contentious. They say Brooklyn wasn't the same after the Dodgers left. I didn't know about that, but it was certainly different around my house. Yankee Stadium was nice, too but it was no Ebbetts field. Anyway, we decided to go to Yankee Stadium. A day at the ballpark with my grandfather, it didn't get any better than that. Kubek, Ford, The Mick. Whack. "That ball is going, going, gone. A home run for Mickey Mantle. Holy Cow!" we'd hear announcer, Phil Rizzuto's call on the transistor radios tuned to the game. The entire stadium jumped to its feet as Mantle rounded the bases.

"Wow, that Mantle can hit. He's better than DiMaggio," a guy in front of us said.

"No way. Joe DiMaggio was the greatest player that ever lived," my grandfather corrected him.

"Plus, he's Italian, right? I added teasing.

"Right," my grandfather confirmed.

Everything seemed correct in the universe that day until I turned around and saw Charlie Giambo with his father a few rows back.

"Oh shit," I said.

I didn't usually curse, my mother didn't allow it, but if ever there was an 'oh shit' moment this was it. My grandfather turned to see the Giambo's. He didn't care for Charlie's father, either. The old axiom was true, 'Like father, like son.' Good and bad.

"Is that kid, Charlie, still bothering you? I can talk to his father."

"No, that's okay, I'm handling it," I tried to assure him.

"Next time he says something punch him right in the nose."

"He's a lot bigger than me, Grandpa."

"Doesn't matter, the only way to get rid of a bully is to punch him in the nose, it's the only language they understand."

My grandfather could see that his solution was not helping.

"Ah, let's not worry about Charlie, let's have fun."

I agreed. And for rest of that day that's what we had. Fun.

There was a cloud that hung over that Sunday's meal. We had fewer people at the table. Uncle Sal and Bernice didn't make the trip in. Uncle Tommy spent the weekend in Boca, Florida to check out a site for a gym, just in case. Aunt Jenny was mysteriously absent. So that left me, my grandfather, grandmother, Aunt Theresa, my mother, and father. Six. We did our best, but it seemed like an awfully small crowd. We had the antipasto as usual. But with Aunt Jenny missing Aunt Theresa finally lifted a finger and helped clear the plates. But something else was missing. Conversation. There wasn't any. Just the sipping of wine followed by "Ahh." It was eerie. Like eating alone. 'Italian Purgatory.'

Finally, my father broke the silence.

"Pop, I spoke to that Chinese guy."

"What Chinese guy?" my grandfather asked.

"The one I told you about. Mr. Lee. He offered us two hundred fifty thousand over the phone. That's fifty thousand more than market value."

"Tell him we're not interested," my grandfather said.

"Pop, we could do a lot of things with that money. Maybe go to Staten Island, set up our operation there."

"I want Joey to be able to work here. In Brooklyn."

My grandfather wasn't about to give up his plans for me. Leave it alone, Dad, I thought to myself. But he couldn't. He could be as stubborn as my grandfather.

"I don't know if Joey is going into the business," my father said.

"What are you talking about? Of course, he's going into the business," my grandfather said.

My father was getting pissed. His face turning red.

"He's not like us. He likes other things.

"What other things?" my grandfather asked.

"Things. Like sports. School. *Writing.*"

My grandfather turned cold. He could have chilled the wine just by holding it.

"Tell the Chinaman we're not selling," my grandfather said firmly.

My father stood up.

"Okay, we're not selling! But don't tell me what Joey can do or not do. I'm his father," my dad said angrily.

My grandfather stood up.

"And I'm his grandfather!"

They stared across the table from each other. My father threw his napkin down on the table and stormed off. My mother stood up and followed him out. I didn't know what to do. Should I follow them out, they were my parents? On the other hand, I hated to go against my grandfather. I looked at my grandmother, then Aunt Theresa and then my grandfather. I stayed at the table.

Chapter 4

A Man Needs to Sweat to Feel Good

Coney Island

I was feeling blue the next day so after school I
headed out to Coney Island to get a hot dog and French
fries at Nathan's Famous. I walked on the boardwalk
smelling the air and listening to the Atlantic Ocean
crash ashore. I couldn't help but think of me and Howie
coming to Coney Island last summer.

Summers in Brooklyn can be incredibly hot. The
European Jews as usual have it figured out; they go to
the Catskill Mountains to cool off. The Syrian Jews, as a

rite of passage, work in bargain discount stores selling electronics, cameras, and binoculars. Italians stay home and sweat. Lucky for me Howie stays home, too. Dr. Schwartz won't leave his patients in the lurch. So last summer Howie and I got to hang out. We went to the beach almost every day. We'd take the BMT subway, Sea Beach line and get off at the last stop. The sign for Coney Island had tons of graffiti so you could barely make it out. But if you couldn't figure it out from all the people wearing bathing suits and carrying beach chairs, umbrellas, picnic baskets, sporting equipment you were in trouble. Why they took all that stuff we couldn't figure out. The trains were crowded, people would have to squeeze in their gear, plus they'd have to lug it all home. Not me and Howie. We travelled light. Two towels and one brown lunch bag each. We rolled the towels in a ball and tucked them under our arms.

We'd always stay by the doors. When the train came to a stop the doors would open, we'd jump out on to the platform, the people would rush in and then we'd reenter the train and stay by the doors again. Not brain surgery but we had to think a little bit. After seven stops we arrived. Coney Island. From the train we could hear the sounds of the ocean waves hitting the seashore. The click, click, of the Cyclone wooden roller coaster as it climbed to the sky with the "Whooos" of anticipation from the riders. Then the blood curdling screams when it dived down. The smell of sea air and cotton candy and French fries tickled our noses. Bliss. Pure bliss.

We were the first to exit the train and we broke into a run up the concrete stairs and through the metal turnstiles. Then we'd hit the street and run all the way to the sand. As we ran, we put on sunscreen. Howie had white skin, he burned easily. I had olive skin, thanks to being Italian, I had a bit of natural protection from the sun's rays. No matter at the end of the day we were both bright red. At the end of the summer a golden tan. We'd remove our Converse sneakers right before we hit the beach so we wouldn't get sand in them. Then we'd head for our spot. The sand was incredibly hot. We'd have to do 'The Sand Dance' as Howie called it, until we got to the spot we wanted to claim for the day. We usually located our spot close to the water. It was always empty there because most people were worried that the tide would come in and wash all their stuff away. We didn't care. Two old beach towels, Mr. Atlantic Ocean, you can have them.

We unfolded the towels, lined them up together, put our Converse sneakers in the corners to hold them down. Then we'd take our lunches out from the brown bags. Howie would have his mom's cheese blintzes and I'd have my grandma's meatball sandwiches. We'd scarf them down right away and, in the background, we'd hear a food vendor dripping with sweat, calling out, "Hot knishes and cold drinks here." Just in case we didn't hear him he repeated it again and again. "Hot knishes and cold drinks here." "Hot knishes and cold drinks here." To shut him up, we'd get one of each and scarfed them down, too. We'd charge into the water.

"Last one in is a rotten egg," we'd say.

Splash, we dove in headfirst into the first wave to hit us. Now common wisdom was you were supposed to wait a minimum of forty-five minutes before you went in the water after eating. But nobody really knew the correct amount of time, so we made up our own times. Cheese blintzes fifteen minutes, meatball sandwiches ten minutes, hot knishes, and cold drink thirty seconds. I figured Howie was the son of a doctor, so if he was willing to take a chance so was I.

We used to swim way out. Way, way out until the people on shore looked like ants, which is what we said every time we swam out there: "The people look like ants." And we'd crack up laughing. If our parents only knew how far out we were they would have had a fit. What would've happened if we had a cramp, or some shark showed up and bit off one of our legs? No lifeguard could swim out in time to save us, and we were okay swimmers, but we certainly were not trained in saving anyone. It was foolish but understandable. Everything was controlled for us back in the neighborhood. Safe. We needed risk in our lives. Adventure. So, we swam far out.

After the beach, we'd hit the penny arcade. We'd throw dimes at glass bottles, shoot hoops on a mini basket, only me, not Howie, throw tennis balls at moving targets, and shooting a water pistol at plastic horses on a pole. We'd shoot a stream of water from a water pistol at a horse to make him go and the steadier the stream the faster the horse went. Whoever hit the finish line first won. The Palumbo men had a lot of experience with this and I usually won, but Howie took it in stride. He knew one day he'd make a lot more money than me and that these games would be trumped. He was right.

We ended the day going on the bumper cars. We'd pick out a car, knowing that they all seemed to go at different speeds so the car you chose was crucial. At least it seemed that way. It probably wasn't. But we made a big deal which car we chose and then hopped in knowing that we made the exact right choice.

"I'm gonna get you, Palumbo."

"Not with this car, Schwartz."

We switched to last names, somehow it made it less personal. We went around the track pretending we were Mickey Rooney in an old movie called 'The Big Wheel' where he plays a race car driver, Billy Cannon Ball Coy. Of course, in the movie Billy Coy wins the big race but not before his car bursts into flames. And yes, he was an underdog. What great fun we had.

The next morning, I walked to school with Howie. I told him what had happened at dinner.

"Nothing like that ever happens at my house. It's a cultural thing. Everyone knows the Italians are hot headed," he said.

"Oh? What about Mr. Resnick? Don't tell me he's the picture of propriety and level headedness?" I asked.

"Good point. You're right. But I must admit I'm afraid of Italians. They're tougher than Jews. Except the

Jews in Israel, they're tougher than anybody," Howie said.

Howie wasn't a fighter, but he could think on his feet. And he had chutzpah. One time we were hanging out on 86th street, at Johnny's Pizza, a popular hangout by the elevated subway called an 'El.' These ghees approached us. They were older, Italian, not from the neighborhood and they were looking to beat up somebody.

"You Jewish?" one of them asked Howie.

"Not if you don't want me to be," Howie said without missing a beat.

"What are you a wise guy?" the hood asked rhetorically. He made a move to grab Howie's pizza and Howie took off. Then I took off. We headed for the 'J'. The ghees in hot pursuit. We ran up the stairs and ran inside. Two pieces of pizza still in our hands. The ghees decided to give up the chase. Howie and I sat in the grandstands in the gym and finished eating our smashed cold pizza.

"I hate ghees. You had a cousin, Eddie. In grade school he used to lie in wait on my route to school and take my lunch money," Howie said.

"Why'd you give it to him?" I asked.

"I was afraid if I didn't give it to him, he'd beat me up. I said to myself, okay I'll give him my 35 cents. But when I become a doctor, and he gets sick and comes to me, I'll refuse to treat him, unless he pays me back all the money he took from me. Plus, interest," Howie said.

"What about not treating him at all?" I asked.

"I couldn't do that. It would go against the Hippocratic oath," Howie said.

Howie was a great guy but sometimes he could get carried away. One time Howie and I were playing basketball in a junior league game at the 'J'. I was the only Italian in the league. I played for the Nobles and we were playing against the dreaded first place Wings. The Nobles were in black uniforms and the Wings in yellow. Coach Zeichick had me guarding Sidney Fishman. He knew I hated Fishman. He was a talented player but a total schmuck. A minute was left on the clock. The Nobles were down by one. The Wings had the ball out of bounds. A player inbounded the ball to Fishman and I'm all over him. He tried a crossover, a move you don't do in that situation. I stuck my hand out and stole the ball. I headed down court as time was about to expire. Howie filled the lane on my left and there was one defender. Sidney Fishman. The crowd was going crazy. Howie's calling for the ball. I saw him. But he was still calling.

"Joey. Joey. I'm free," he said all excited.

Fishman was between us, not sure who to defend.

"Stop the ball," his coach, Normie Bean, yelled out.

Fishman jumped in front of me. Two seconds left now. I took the ball and threw it behind my back to Howie. This was a rarity at the time, except for Bob Cousy, who was in the N.B.A. The crowd went wild, roaring in delight. Howie put out his hands to grab the ball. It went right through his fingers.

"Ohhh," the crowd groaned.

We lost by one point.

In the locker room after the game Howie was inconsolable.

"I cost us the game. My life for all intents and purposes is over. Put a bag over my head. I can win the Nobel Prize for medicine and they'll say at the last second:

"Wait, aren't you the guy who missed that behind the back pass from your best friend? You cost your team the game. Sorry, I have to take this back," Howie recited.

Like I said, Howie could get carried away sometimes, but usually he'd recover, but for some reason that pass got to him and from that day forward Howard Steven Schwartz did not touch a basketball.

As we walked through Seth Low Park to the school that day, I remembered what I wanted to ask Howie:

"In Jewish homes, do people keep secrets from each other?"

"You're kidding, right? he said. "In Jewish homes keeping secrets is a way of life. And forget about telling the truth. Anything the least bit dicey gets shoved under the rug. I saw my Uncle Morty once in his house wearing a dress. But would anybody tell me the truth? Hell no. He's in a play rehearsing his part as a woman. Trouble is my uncle is no more of an actor than I am. Nobody tells the truth in Jewish families. Nobody. That's how we stay together."

Hmm, an interesting take.

We arrived at school and went our separate paths. But I was feeling better knowing my family wasn't the only ones who stretched the truth or kept secrets. But I didn't like hearing that story about my cousin, Eddie. If I knew Eddie was bullying Howie, I would have stopped him. I should have known. Where was I? How did I miss so much? I needed to somehow get even.

I made up my mind the next time Charlie bothered me I was going to punch him in the nose. Just like my grandfather told me to do. What I didn't realize was I'd get my chance so soon. Charlie and his boys were hanging out on the path waiting for me.

"Hey, Joey, how can you afford to go to the movies if your grandfather's going bankrupt?" Charlie asked.

"He is not, Charlie," I answered.

"Then when is he going to pay his bill to my father?" he asked.

"Get out of my way," I demanded.

"Make me," he said, the old Brooklyn standard challenge.

Suddenly when faced with Charlie I wasn't as brave as I thought I'd be. In fact, I was scared shitless. This guy was a lot bigger than me. I didn't even know if I could reach his nose, much less punch it. Charlie saw my hesitation and began to cluck like a chicken. "Cluck, cluck, cluck, cluck, cluck."

I couldn't take it. I went over and pushed him. Okay, it wasn't a punch, but a push can sometimes be quite effective.

"Did you push me? Did he just push me? He pushed me, right?" Howie asked his friends. The brain trust agreed, I pushed him. A sin punishable by death in bully land. Charlie handed his notebook to his friend and he pushed me back. Hard. I fell back a few feet. I stared at Charlie.

"What are you going to do, huh? Punch me in the nose?" Charlie asked.

Damn right I was. I made a fist, wound up, and bam hit him right in the old schnozzol as Jimmy Durante used to say. Charlie was in shock. This pipsqueak actually had the nerve to hit him. Then the unthinkable happened. He saw blood. Uh oh. Charlie began throwing punches wildly, and I started punching back. We were toe to toe. Charlie was getting the best of it. His reach was twice mine. Then I executed a move I saw Antonio Rocca use against Bruno Sanmartino that I learned watching professional wrestling with my grandfather. I faked high and went low. I grabbed his legs and brought him to the ground. I got on top of him and began wailing away. A big crowd gathered cheering me on.

"Joey. Joey. Joey. Joey."

If ever there was an underdog, I was it. I was holding my own though. But I knew it wouldn't last. Charlie began kicking me.

"Hey kicking's not allowed," someone said.

Charlie was not about to follow the Marquis De Queensberry rules. His reputation was at stake. He bit me on the leg. I bit him back on his leg. Tit for tat. We jumped at each other and rolled around and around. Mr. Hunt came over and tried to break us up.

"Stop it you two! I said, stop it!" he demanded.

He pulled Charlie off me.

"In my office. Now!!" he ordered us.

We went into Mr. Hunt's office. The nameplate front and center on his desk. 'Dean.' Not good. Charlie and I settled into our respective chairs. Charlie put his feet up on Mr. Hunt's desk. Mr. Hunt shot him a look. He returned his feet to the floor. I was ahead on points.

"He started it," Charlie said beating me to the punch.

"No, he started it," I shot back.

Mr. Hunt wanted to know what we were arguing about. We both started talking at once. Mr. Hunt held up his hand. He pointed to me. I didn't consider this ratting; this came under the category of defending oneself.

"Charlie said my grandfather is going bankrupt," I said.

"He is," said Charlie.

"I see. Look, the problem is not whether he is or isn't going bankrupt, the problem is it's a private matter. Not to be spoken in public," Mr. Hunt explained.

Hey, this guy is good, I thought.

"Does that make sense to you, Charles? How such a sensitive subject might hurt Joseph's feelings?" he asked.

Charlie had this puzzled look on his face. Who is this guy? He managed to mumble: "I guess."

"You guess?" Mr. Hunt asked.

"I don't have to answer no more questions unless my lawyer's present," Charlie uttered.

Mr. Hunt looked at him in disbelief. Then he meted out his punishment.

"One demerit each for fighting. One more and you'll be suspended," he said.

He waited for his words to sink in.

"Can I go now?" Charlie asked.

"Yes, you can go," Mr. Hunt said.

Charlie shot up like a cannonball and ran out. Mr. Hunt looked at me. Just shook his head. He knew what

I was up against, what could he say. We both knew that this wouldn't be the end of it. Charlie cared about his rep and having some little guy get the best of him or at least draw blood was something he couldn't live with. I had to keep my guard up.

Mr. Hunt walked me to the door, wished me good luck. Then he tried to change the subject.

"Have you given any thought about going to college?" he asked.

"I have but the whole thing is kind of overwhelming," I answered.

"Why not see Mr. Sandler, the guidance counselor? Maybe he can help you?" he suggested.

"Okay," I said, "maybe I will. Thanks."

The next day I marched myself right over to Mr. Sandler's office. I knocked on the door.

"Come in," I heard from the other side of the door.

I walked in and there he sat at his desk, behind the nameplate reading, Bruce Sandler, Guidance Counselor. Dressed a bit rumpled, he had the look of a man who had been at his job too long. I had seen him around school but had never actually talked to him. I was a little nervous. Okay, a lot nervous. When I got that way, I talked as if I had to go pee. I blurted out in one long sentence: "Hi-Mr.-Sandler-I-was-hoping-you-might-be-able-to-help-me-Mr. Hunt-thinks-I-should-go-to-college-and-so-does-Mrs.- Scalise-and-Becky's-dad-but-I'm-not-so-sure-no-one-in- my-family-has-gone-to-college-unless-you-count-my- cousin-Rosemary-but-she's-a-girl-so-I-was-wondering-what-you-think? (then slow) About going to college."

"And you are?" he asked.

"Joey. Joey Palumbo. Class 9-14," I said

"Oh. One of them. Sit down, Joseph. Please," he said.

I sat in a chair opposite his.

"Palumbo. Any relation to Vincent Palumbo?" he wondered.

"He's my grandfather," I proudly said.

"Really? Wow, I am in awe then," he said, "your grandfather remodeled my whole house. What a craftsman. So, what brings you here?"

"I need some guidance whether I should go to college," I shortened my spiel.

He got up and closed the door. Then he returned to his chair.

"You know how a zebra wishes he were a horse. But the problem is he can't get rid of his stripes? You see where I'm going?" Sandler asked.

"No, not really," I answered.

"You'd be going against a biological imperative. Think about it, your sink is stopped up, who do you call? A Kagan? A Weinstein? A Goldberg? I don't think so. But you need your taxes done, some legal advice, a doctor, bingo, you got your man. If I were you, I'd finish high school and go into my grandfather's business. Life is about choices, and sometimes the best choice is right in front of you. Nice talking to you Joseph and say hello to your grandfather for me. You're one lucky boy," he said.

I got up and left. I thought to myself, of course, what was I thinking. Construction. It's in my DNA. Boy that was a relief. Now I could go on with my life.

That afternoon my grandfather wanted me to go someplace with him. Looking back, it was the beginning of my schooling in construction. I had the best teacher in the world. I decided not to bring up the fight with Charlie, my grandfather had enough on his plate. He had his radio set on the opera station as usual, but he wasn't singing along that day. Opera was one of his passions. Italian opera, of course. Puccini, Verdi, Donizetti, give him a vowel at the end, he loved the composer. Leoncavallo was his favorite. Pagliacci was his favorite opera. Vesti La Giubba was his favorite song from that opera. The song was about a clown who discovers his wife has been unfaithful to him, but nevertheless he must prepare for his performance as Pagliacci. The show must go on. And when Enrico Caruso sang Vesti La Giubba on the radio fuhgeddaboudit, my grandfather sang along with him at the top of his lungs. Sometimes I'd join him.

"Ridi Pagliacci, sul tuo amore! Ridi del duol che tavelena il cor!" we'd sing together.

My Italian was pretty good from hanging out with Papa Nunzio. But today when Caruso came on the radio, my grandfather showed no emotion. I was in no mood to go solo. We just stared ahead. We finally arrived at our destination. Kings Highway and East 35th. I had been there once before to pick up drawings. This was where Max Rotter's office was. Max was an architect. And Palumbo & Son did most of his jobs. At least they used to. My grandfather parked the truck at a meter, he put some change in the slot and we walked toward the office.

I had to keep up with him, he seemed to forget I was there the closer we got to Max's office. We went inside. There were moving boxes everywhere. I thought to myself what's going on and why was I there? Max came out and greeted my grandfather warmly, with respect. He reached over and tussled my hair.

"Hey Joe, what's happening?" he asked me.

Max was hip, today, worldly, everything my grandfather wasn't. He had these incredibly long fingers, the fingers of a basketball player or an artist. He was both. He had played for Pratt Institute. He averaged eighteen a game. Eighteen rebounds. I knew he had a tryout with the Knicks. But he didn't make it. He 'drifted into architecture' they said in the neighborhood. In Bensonhurst, sports was king, everything else secondary. If you played ball and didn't make it and took up medicine you'd hear, "That Jonas Salk, he didn't make the NBA, so he drifted into medicine." Funny but crazy at the same time.

"How do you think the Knicks will do this year, Joe?" Max asked me. But before I could answer he ushered us into his office.

"Find some chairs if you can," he said.

We all sat down. My grandfather took off his hat, cradled it in those meat cleaver hands in front of him. It was then I knew what my grandfather was doing there. He was looking for work, hat in hand. Begging for work. Vincent Nunzio Palumbo. I wanted to cry. Max was nervous, fidgety.

"Excuse the mess, I'm moving the office to Staten Island," he said.

My grandfather just sat there.

"But I already told you that on the phone." Max said.

"I was hoping maybe you had something for us. We haven't heard from you in a while," my grandfather said.

"Yeah, well the nature of my work has changed. I'm no longer doing custom work. Knock it out, that's what they want nowadays. You gotta change with the times, isn't that what they say, Joey?" he asked me to try to bring me in to the conversation.

"I guess," I said not knowing what to say.

"If something comes up in Staten Island maybe you can give us a call?" my grandfather asked.

"I will. Definitely. I will." Max answered.

Even I knew he had no intention of doing that.

"Well, I'd like to sit around and shoot the breeze but I gotta be out of here by tomorrow," Max said, and he stood up. We were getting the bum's rush. My grandfather stood up. He looked around the office.

"Can I use your bathroom?" my grandfather asked.

"Sure, Vince. Sure. You know where it is," he said.

My grandfather headed for the bathroom. Max knew how difficult this was for him. For me. He tried to soften the blow.

"You know, your grandfather built this office for me. What a builder, every detail executed precisely. Look at that ceiling molding. Look at those joints. They broke the mold when they made men like him, they broke the mold," he said.

I stood there. I just had my first lesson in construction humiliation 101. We left the office and headed for the truck. A parking ticket was under the windshield wiper. Not a good day for the Palumbos. My grandfather grabbed that ticket and yelled out a loud, "Fuck." I think that was the first time I had heard him use the 'F' word in front of me. My grandmother frowned on cursing.

We got in the pick-up and headed home. But before we got home, we drove to the Washington cemetery on

McDonald Avenue where my grandfather gave me driving lessons in his pick-up truck. I was getting pretty good. Clutch, shift, release, gas. What's so hard?

We had to do it on the sly because my parents would plotz. Before we practiced driving, we would always pay our respects to Papa Nunzio. There was a flower shop nearby called The Flower Shop, what else, and we'd pick out some red roses and leave them on his grave. Sometimes I'd read the Italian newspaper to his headstone. It wasn't the same though.

We practiced along the street that hugs the cemetery because it was a quiet street. I was behind the wheel. I moved the seat way forward so I could reach the pedals.

"This is cool, Grandpa. And to think I'm only fifteen." I couldn't help but brag.

"I was ten when I learned to drive," he bragged.

"Ten? That's young, even for you," I said.

"Papa Nunzio taught me. At the lumber yard. We'd pick out the wood together inside and when he went to pay for it, I'd drive the truck from the parking lot to the loading dock so he could load it. He'd show me how to tie it off with rope, so it didn't shift when we were on the road. It got to where he let me tie it off. I taught you, right?" he asked.

"Right, Grandpa," I said.

Knowing different types of rope knots always held this strange fascination for me. One of the main reasons I joined the Boy Scouts. Bowline, slip knot, timber hitch, I could do them all. Just then a car turned the corner. Uh oh.

"It's okay. Just go slow," he warned me.

The car got closer.

"Careful, careful," he said.

I gripped the steering wheel tight. Now the car was getting close. Clutch, shift, release, gas. Now it was just a few feet away. I saw another kid being taught to drive by his grandfather. And he was doing clutch, shift, release, gas. Now I panicked. The kid saw me, and he panicked.

"Joey!!" my grandfather yelled out.

Bang, crash. Boom.

"Oh shit," I said.

I just sat there. My driving world had come to a crashing end.

"Sit tight," my grandfather said.

He went over to the other car. The other old guy got out of his car. I didn't know what to expect. This was a bad day for the family, and I made it worse. I felt terrible. I was waiting for the exchange of licenses, registration, insurance companies. Maybe fisticuffs. I had seen it often enough. I had even experienced it once with Papa Nunzio before they took his license away. But the men just talked. The only thing they exchanged were words. The power of words. Impressive. Then I saw my grandfather pat him on the back, and the men shook hands. What's going on I wondered? Then my grandfather came back to his car.

"Nice Italian man. That's enough driving for today. Let's go home," he said.

We did. My grandfather drove. When we got home, we went to the basement to sort wine. We did this a lot. Moving the bottles to bring the older years forward and put the newer batch in the back. My grandfather would get on the ladder and I'd hold it. Lately he had a hard time seeing the numbers. He handed me a bottle.

"What year, Joey?" he asked.

"1956, Grandpa," I answered.

I passed it back up. He took the bottle and put it in the rack. It was a good system. Then he descended the ladder as I held it tight. I looked on the table.

"Oops, we forgot one," I said.

"What year?" he asked.

"1954," I said.

"Forget it," he said.

I put the wine back on the wooden table. It was like a picnic table with benches. He had just 'knocked it out' from some scrap lumber at the yard. My grandfather could 'knock out' anything made of wood. I saw a tree, he saw a bookcase, maybe a couple of chairs. My father had the gift, too. The jury was still out on me.

My grandfather sat at the table. He dusted some cake crumbs off it, which were 'ruining' his creation. I sat across from him. We stared at the bottle. He looked around to see if the coast was clear. Not an authority figure in sight.

"You want some?" he asked.

"Sure," I said.

He took out his Swiss Army knife, the kind with a million assorted blades. He had some trouble pulling out the corkscrew.

"Joey, get a couple of glasses, please," he said.

I went over to a cabinet and pulled out a couple of wine glasses. Plastic. The basement set. I put them on the table. He poured himself some wine, then poured some for me. It was like it was all happening in slow motion.

Then we clinked glasses.

"Salud," we said in unison.

My grandfather took a sip. I followed with my own sip.

"Ahh," he said, "A day without wine..

"..is a day without sun," I finished the saying.

He smiled. He had put the day's travails behind him and was just enjoying the moment with me. Then he must've remembered I wasn't supposed to be drinking.

"Don't tell your parents," he said.

I made my usual sign of zipping my lips.

"Good boy," he said.

He then picked up the Swiss Army knife and put back the corkscrew. I loved that knife. If only I was allowed to have one.

"You want it?" my grandfather asked. "It can be an early birthday present."

"Sure," I said.

He handed it over to me.

I stared at the knife in my hand. Wow.

"Thanks, Grandpa."

"Every builder has to have a good Swiss Army knife. You put it away, in your pocket," he said.

I did, quickly. Then my grandfather held up his glass in a toast.

"To the day when you come into the business," he said.

We clinked glasses again.

"Salud," we both said.

My grandfather leaned over and grabbed a book resting on the card table behind him. He put on his reading glasses.

"I want to read you something," he said.

He took off his reading glasses and whipped out his handkerchief to clean them. I could tell it was an annoyance to him, but he was at the age now where he had to wear them. As he was cleaning them, I was thinking hearing aids can't be too far behind. These things were inherited. Papa Nunzio wore hearing aids. His hands were too unsteady to put the batteries in, so I did it for him.

My grandfather wasn't there yet. Just the glasses.

"You read it. My eyes are not so good for reading anymore," he admitted.

He handed me the book. I turned to a bookmarked page. Then I read it out loud.

"WHEN we build, let us think that we build forever. Let it not be for present delight nor for present use alone. Let it be such work as our descendants will thank us for; and let us think as we lay stone on stone, that a time is to come when those stones will be held sacred because our hands have touched them, and that men will say, as they look upon the labor and wrought substance of them, "See! This our father did for us."

I closed the book.

"Now that's what I call a great writer," I said. I looked at the jacket.

"Huh, John Ruskin. Not even Italian," I said amazed.

"Could be," my grandfather said.

"Nah, his name doesn't end in a vowel," I said.

"Maybe they made him change it for the book?" he wondered.

"I don't think so, Grandpa," I said.

I returned the book to him. He held up the book, admiring its content.

"The subject was good, too. You need a good subject to be a good writer," he said.

He placed the book on the table behind him.

"Joey, being a builder is a good life for a man. At the end of the day you can see what you've done. And you sweat. A man needs to sweat to feel good. Capisce?"

"Capisce," I said.

Only this time I meant it. I already had a Swiss Army knife. A Skil saw couldn't be far behind. Besides I wasn't so sure I could be a writer now. I couldn't write as good as John Ruskin. What would be the point?

I had lost track of the time. When I finally went upstairs, I found my mother pacing.

"Where were you?" she frantically asked. "We were worried sick."

"I was with Grandpa," I said.

"All day?" she asked.

"He's teaching me the business," I said.

Then she put her nose by my mouth.

"What's that I smell?" she wondered.

I pulled my face back. This surely came under the heading of not respecting a person's privacy.

"Nothing," I said, hoping this parental inquisition would stop.

She smelled me again.

"It's wine," she said. Then turning to my father, "Can you believe this?"

My father stepped in. He knew who was to blame.

"Joey, I told you no wine," he said.

"I know, I know. It was just a few sips. We were celebrating the day I come into the business," I said.

"Well next time celebrate it another way," he said. "Look, Joe, your mother got a call from school," he said.

"Charlie started it, Dad," I said.

"That's no reason to fight. I told you to ignore him," he said.

"You fought in the Army. In fact, you killed people. Didn't you?" I asked.

"That was different. I had no choice," he said.

"What happened there? What happened that you don't want to talk about?" I asked.

"Never mind me. This is about you. Use your words, Joey. You want to be a writer, use your words," he said.

"Sometimes words aren't enough," I said starting to tear up.

My mother hated to see me cry. From when I was a toddler. She came over to me to explain.

"What your father means is there's always a way to avoid fighting. If somebody is giving you a hard time at school, you tell your teachers. Or us. Now go do your homework. You can use my office," she offered.

I went in my mother's office. I took out my term paper and started to write. But nothing good was coming out. I crumpled up the paper, put my head down on the desk and cried.

Chapter 5

Reaching Second Base

Marboro Theater

I was feeling guilty about not spending enough time with my father, so I invited him to a movie. I had to do a little coaxing to get him to go, but he usually enjoyed himself once he was inside the theater. My grandmother gave us sausage sandwiches that we had to sneak in.

The Marboro was the movie theatre of choice. A few thousand seats. Huge. About 1250 below in orchestra seating and about 750 in the balcony. The Jewish kids sat in the orchestra seats and the Italians sat in the balcony. The Jews watched the films. And the Italians? Well they hooted and hollered, talked back to the screen, threw spitballs at each other, and the top row was called, 'The make out row,' so that's what they did.

My father and I sneaked our sandwiches in. We sat below, embarrassed at what might be going on above. Speaking of sneaking in, another Bensonhurst tradition happened at the theater. Several boys would pay their way into the theater and then soon after the movie began playing and it was pitch black they would suddenly push open a few side exit doors from the inside and a bunch of kids would come pouring in from outside yelling "Geronimo" at the top of their lungs. Mary, the elderly matron, flashlight at the ready, did her best to catch at least some of them but the kids were too quick. They would quickly disperse throughout the theatre and then sit quietly with their hands folded until the commotion passed. It happened every Saturday like clockwork. The manager, Murray, could have prevented it by adding security but he chose not to. It became part of the show.

My father and I settled in after the excitement and waited for the film. It was usually preceded by black and white newsreels, which were documentary clips of current events. That day they had a newsreel of troops coming home from Vietnam. My father just stared straight ahead with a glazed look as the balcony whooped and hollered their heads off. It made me sad, though. I hated to see him that way.

My spirits did pick up though because that day my favorite movie of all time was playing. 'A Thousand Clowns.' It was a story about a free-spirited Jewish uncle, played by Jason Robards, who was taking care of his genius nephew in a one room apartment. Two social workers wanted to remove the boy from such an 'unwholesome' environment. It took place in Manhattan.

I couldn't get enough of this movie. I loved everything about it, the writing, the acting, the setting. I had heard a lot about Manhattan but had never actually been there. "It's dangerous. Too far. Plus, the food's better in Brooklyn. Achtooie on Manhattan."

Wait, I did go to Manhattan. Once. My parents took me for my Communion. We saw the Rockettes at Radio City Music Hall. But I was whisked in and out of there so fast I hardly saw anything. They were afraid Manhattan might stick. I was relegated to watching Manhattan on film. And this movie was filmed all over

Manhattan. I could remember entering the theatre for my seventh time to see the film just as my Aunt Gigi was coming out.

"Don't bother," she said.

"I'm here, I might as well go in," I said smiling.

We watched the film and I could see it picked up my father's spirits. The power of a good film. Vietnam, the business, were all forgotten for that one Saturday.

The next morning, I got up before everyone else which I didn't do often. But that day I needed less stress in my life, so I tuned in to the TV show I watched to accomplish that task. The Debbie Drake Show. The exercise lady. Debbie was the female version of Jack LaLanne. She had short cropped blond hair, and a cute perky face kinda like Mary Tyler Moore. She wore a tan leotard that showed off her perfect body. It had a white choir boy collar trying to diminish her sexiness. It didn't work. Her chest was so well formed it cast a shadow on her leotard. Her legs were long, but she was still able to touch the floor with her palms. She did her exercises on a carpet in front of a rather dreary living room set. Perhaps they wanted to give the impression Debbie was like regular folk. She wasn't. I was addicted to the show. Her.

"Bend over and back and up. Back and up. Back and up. Back and up. And back and up," she instructed.

I never did any of the exercises. I knew them all by heart, but I never left my bed. Debbie was my little secret. Except for Howie. He knew. But we made a pact, he wouldn't tell anybody about Debbie, and I wouldn't ever mention that dropped behind the back pass. Seemed like a fair trade. We didn't sign anything, but Howie's word was as good as gold.

Debbie Drake personified the ideal woman to me. She was even smart like Becky. She produced and wrote her own show. She was an older version of Becky. I had no illusions. She was a grown-up woman and I was a kid. Case closed.

I met Becky at the usual spot on Monday morning and we walked to school together. I was unconsciously whistling the Debbie Drake theme song.

"You're in a good mood today," Becky said.

"Yes, I guess I am," I said.

"Does Debbie Drake have something to do with it?" she asked.

"Who?" I asked playing dumb.

"You know, the exercise lady? I watched her show," Becky said.

"You did?" I asked.

"Yeah, she's pretty," she said.

"She's okay, if you like the perky type," I said.

"It's okay, Joey, the female form is to be admired. You have nothing to be embarrassed about. Or ashamed," she instructed me.

That was the thing about Becky, she was always ahead of me. In all matters. Except movies and mattresses. I knew more about those subjects than her. Everything else I was waay behind. We reached our destination and before we separated to go to our respective classes, she held my arm.

"How about we take in a movie on Saturday?" she proposed.

"Sure," I said, "What's playing?"

"It doesn't matter. Bye," she said.

And she was gone.

Hmm. What did she mean it doesn't matter? That was a strange thing to say. How did she know about Debbie Drake? It had to be Howie. He was the only person who knew. But that wasn't like him. Or was it? He always liked Becky. Maybe he wanted to sabotage our relationship so he could move in for the kill. I needed to sort it out.

I still had some time before class, so I went to a dirt area, where there used to be grass. There were benches there, a concrete curved base with wooden slats for seats. The ninth grade "ghees" hung out there. They were our Italian tough guys. Our J.D.'s. Their girlfriends were known as "gheetresses". These words are not in the dictionary so don't bother to look them up. The 'ghees' left me and the other athletes alone. They respected kids that could play sports. Part of the 'ghee' code of ethics. They were more into fashion. Peg pants, pointed shoes, hair pulled back, a snarl on their faces, and they kept their cigs in shirt sleeves that were rolled up exposing their arms.

They weren't there that day. Who knows why? Usually when that happened it meant they had to attend a wedding or a christening for a baby of one of the "gheetresses." It didn't matter to me; I was just happy they weren't there so I could play 'Land'.

I pulled out my Swiss Army knife and started to draw a rectangle in the dirt. Land was usually played by two people and the object was to throw a knife into the ground and wherever it landed you'd carve a line in the dirt 'acquiring' that piece of land. It was one of the many games that were passed down from older kids to younger kids. I often wondered who the first person was to come up with the street games. Howie said it was his Uncle Sol, he came up with all the street games. Triangle, box ball, stoop ball, hit the penny, stickball, punch ball, Johnny on the pony, King Queen, all Uncle Sol. The games were simple, creative and the best thing, free. No schedules, no play dates, no babying in those days. Much easier on the parents. You fed your kid breakfast, opened the door and your kid started his day. Then he came home, you fed him dinner, and tucked him in at night. In between was up to him. In a way we raised each other. Got our information from each other, got our misinformation from each other. There was plenty of that. Two worlds, street life and family life. The kids of Bensonhurst did their best to keep them separate.

As I played land I thought about Howie. Why did he tell Becky about Debbie Drake? He must've had a reason. I'd find out sooner or later. For now, I just wanted to be alone with my thoughts. Until, you guessed it, Charlie Giambo showed up. I had just thrown my knife in the dirt. It stuck straight up in the air. I was about to pull it out of the dirt when Charlie beat me to it.

"Hey, nice knife," he said.

"Give that back to me," I demanded.

I was in no mood to play around. Charlie turned his back on me and held the knife out of my reach.

"He shouldn't have a knife, right guys? He's too young," Charlie said.

"Yeah, way too young," the brain trust agreed.

I tried to grab it back.

"You give that back to me," I said trying to take back my knife.

Charlie held it out of my reach, spinning in circles like a dog with a frisbee does to another dog trying to get it. I was getting pissed.

"You give that back to me or..."

"Or what? You'll punch me in the nose?" Charlie said.

"I'll tell Mr. Hunt you're a big bully," I said.

"Rat on me? You'd rat on me, Palumbo?" he questioned my Brooklyn moral code.

"My father says it's not ratting if you're correcting bad behavior," I mimicked what my father had told me.

"Yeah, well you're committing bad behavior by bringing a knife to school in the first place," Charlie said, proud of himself for making such an intelligent word connection.

"Give it back, Charlie, my grandfather gave me that knife," I said as I tried to get it.

"Your grandfather is going broke he shouldn't be giving things away," Charlie said as he avoided my grasp.

"Drop dead. Give it back," I said.

Mr. Hunt was talking with one of the boys about ten feet away. Charlie thought a moment, then handed me the knife back. I was surprised for a moment at this act of generosity. But then Charlie shouted out to Mr. Hunt.

"Mr. Hunt... Mr. Hunt..."

Mr. Hunt turned to us.

"Joey has a knife!" Charlie shouted.

Then he pointed to me holding the knife. It seemed the entire student body turned to see me holding that knife. Mr. Hunt came rushing over. I tried to explain what had happened. But it was my word against Charlie's and the fact that Mr. Hunt saw me with the knife and all the kids outside saw me meant he had to act. Next thing I knew I was in Mr. Hunt's office. My mother and father were there, and the knife was resting on Mr. Hunt's desk. Mr. Hunt explained the school rules that bringing weapons to school was strictly forbidden. The fact I already had one demerit; two demerits meant immediate expulsion.

My mother, my staunchest defender spoke up.

"I can assure you that we are as upset as you are," she said.

"Joey's a smart boy, he knows bringing a weapon to school is not allowed," Mr. Hunt said.

I piped up, doing my best Perry Mason impression:

"It's not a weapon. It's a tool. One that every good builder has. Being a builder is a good life for a man. At the end of the day you can see what you've done. And you sweat. A man needs to sweat to feel good."

From their silence I realized I might have laid it on a little too thick. My father, who seemed stunned by the whole fiasco finally spoke up.

"Joey, did Grandpa give you this knife?" he asked.

"Uh, no. I found it," I fibbed.

"Don't lie, son," he said.

I didn't want to get my grandfather in trouble, but I hated to lie to my father.

"Son, tell the truth," he said to me.

"Yeah, he gave it to me," I admitted, my eyes looked down toward the floor.

I would've made a terrible captive. No need for water torture, or the rack, or lashes with a whip, just ask me to tell the truth and I'll tell it to you. Then Mr. Hunt spoke next. The judge and jury.

"I'm sorry, but I have no other choice but to suspend Joey for one month," he said.

"One month?" my mother exclaimed.

Having had some success in 'The Real Estate' negotiating, she had to give it a try. One month was the offer, she was going to present her counteroffer.

"What if Joey promises to never do it again? And he does work around the school like cleaning up the gym, or cleaning the erasers, bathrooms, whatever," she offered.

"I'm sorry. One month," Mr. Hunt said. His best and final offer. I heard an imaginary gavel. Next case.

Mr. Hunt handed the knife to my father. He stared at it. He didn't say anything, put it in his pocket. I felt like crawling in a cave. Maybe go back to Sicily. Start all over. Learn to fish. That's it, I thought, I'll be a fisherman. On the way home I just sat in the back of my mother's car. A 1962 Pontiac. A baby blue convertible. The one she used to drive clients around to look at houses. But my father was driving today. And he was pissed.

"This is no way to live," he said.

My mother tried to ease the situation.

"Look, nobody got hurt. That's the main thing. No mother in the house, a crazy father, no wonder that kid, Charlie, is a problem," my mother, the shrink said.

"It's not Charlie I have a problem with," my father fumed. Uh oh.

We drove up to the curb in front of the house. I thought I was a goner. House arrest, no TV, no grandma lunches, one Yankee Doodle every two weeks. And forget about Sunday dinner. That for sure was history. My father exited the car, walked past the magnolia tree and into the house. My mother and I looked at each other. Where is he going? He headed for the basement. We followed him. He stomped down the stairs. We figured out who was the unlucky recipient of his wrath. My grandfather.

Too late to warn him, we hung at the top of the stairs. Out of view, but where we could hear everything. Listening Toms, we were. My father reached the basement floor. My grandfather quickly put away something he was sanding.

"I want you to take this back," my father said.

He threw the knife on the table! My mother and I shared a look. We didn't know this guy anymore and what he might be capable of doing.

"The school is making a big deal over nothing," my grandfather said.

"It's not the school. It's you. I don't want you giving Joey knives. He's too young," my father said.

"It's a pocketknife for Chrissakes. A pocketknife never hurt anyone," my grandfather insisted.

"Is that right?" my father said.

"I was eight years old when my father gave me my first pocketknife," my grandfather said.

"I don't care if you were five. No more knives. No more wine. No more him driving your truck. I know what's going on, I'm not blind," my father said.

"You'll make him soft, Danny," my grandfather said.

"Soft is good. There's too much 'hard' in the world," my father said.

"A boy needs to learn to become a man," my grandfather preached.

"Not yet he doesn't." My father got two inches from my grandfather's face.

"You don't get it, do you? You know how Gina and I feel, and you just go ahead and do what you want," my father said.

"Because I'm right! And you two are wrong!" my grandfather barked.

My father grabbed the knife. He held it up as if he was going to strike. Then he threw it to the ground and stormed off.

My father climbed back up the stairs. As he passed me and my mother he said:

"I can't take this anymore. I'm suffocating here."

My mother and I were very worried about my father and what he might do. Run away like Uncle Paul. Jump off the six-story apartment building on 75th street like other distraught people had done. From that night on we watched my father closely.

Being home from school got boring after a while but I did have the term paper to do. But it's hard to a do a paper on someone if that someone doesn't want to talk about himself. At least I had the movie with Becky on Saturday. I looked up what was playing. "Cat Ballou" with Lee Marvin. Although Becky said it didn't matter, whatever that means.

Saturday finally arrived. Becky sometimes went to temple Saturday mornings. Which brings up another subject - religion. The European Jews weren't very religious for the most part. The Sephardic Jews were much more observant. They had their own synagogues. The very Orthodox "black hats" Jews started to come into the neighborhood and infiltrated the Sephardic community with more stringent rules, like women and men couldn't sit together during a service.

We weren't very religious in my house. Except for Aunt Theresa and we figured she went to church enough for all of us. One of the reasons the Italians didn't go to Catholic mass was they didn't like that the priests were all Irish. In fact, at the time most of the church hierarchy was Irish. Cardinal Spellman was at the peak of his power. The saying went, "When Spellman spoke people and politicians listened." But not the Italians. The Italians had trouble with authority figures. Politicians, teachers, cops. That was one of the reasons the Mafia came about. They made their own hierarchy. Settled things among themselves. But the family did say a prayer every Sunday before we ate. We believed in

God and celebrated all the Catholic holidays. Easter, Christmas, Passover, just checking to see if you are paying attention. I had my communion and confirmation; Uncle Joe was chosen as my godfather. He was married to my father's sister, Aunt Josie. Aunt Josie was a sweetheart. You bought a suit that was too long, Aunt Josie would hem it. A hole in your sock, she was the one you'd take it to. She was also good at fixing problems of the heart. But only for the girls. The boys were on their own. Besides, expressing personal problems was a sign of weakness. At least that is what the macho Italians thought. We suffered in silence until it boiled over and someone got belted. A tough way to live and not recommended for the general population.

I liked Uncle Joe a lot. But I probably would've chosen Uncle Frankie. Uncle Frankie was an artist. Oils. He was pretty good, but he always seemed to be working on this one painting of the Madonna and Child. Couldn't get it right, I guessed. Or maybe he couldn't afford to buy another canvas. But the best thing about Uncle Frankie was he was my basketball mentor. He taught me how to dribble with both hands, do a no-look pass and most importantly how to hit a set shot with a nerf basketball with my eyes closed. But basketball aside Uncle Joe was probably the better role model and that's why he was chosen. I loved Uncle Joe, but I couldn't understand what he was saying sometimes. He was born in Sicily and spoke broken English. He called air conditioning "air condish," he called my father, "slow mosh," meaning slow motion, because he moved slow and 'chuch' for church. When the family did go to 'chuch' it was St. Athanasius on 61st Street and 21st Ave. Aunt Theresa's 'chuch' of choice. I vividly remember going there for catechism. Every Wednesday at 2 PM the Catholic kids left their classes to study for their confirmation. In my Italian class that meant everybody. Except Heshie Hershcovitz, our only Jew. Heshie stayed and read sports magazines. Staying 'sports current' was a must in Brooklyn. Many an hour was spent on street corners and in soda shops talking about sports. We knew batting averages, R.B.I. totals, points per game, rebounds, assists, everything. We could talk about potential trades, weighing the pros and cons for both teams. And we knew what we were talking about. Especially Heshie. He was a sports genius, but the craziest thing, he could barely write his name. I fed him answers on standardized tests in exchange for the latest sports information, betting lines, gossip, that sort of thing. He knew about potential trades before the general managers did. Rumor had it that later in his life Las Vegas banned him from betting, he was winning too much. Then he was found in the trunk of a car. He got in with the wrong crowd. I sometimes wondered if Heshie could've made better use of his time than just focusing on sports. Probably not.

Although Becky went to temple, she wasn't very religious either. She was a reform Jew, not conservative or Orthodox. Although she had a few cousins who were. And they most of all weren't happy she was seeing a goy. Me. Anyway, it was Saturday, so I met Becky at the Marboro. She looked nice, having just come from temple. I thought I'd emphasize the point.

"Hi, Becky, you look nice."

"You don't look so bad yourself, big boy," she said in her best Mae West voice.

With the greetings and salutations behind us, we headed to the ticket booth.

"I got it," she said.

"Huh? What about going Dutch?" I asked.

"No, today is my treat," she insisted.

Hey, fine by me. I didn't have much money back then.

We went inside, took our seats. In the orchestra section as usual. We sat through the usual previews, newsreels, cartoons and finally, finally the movie came on to cheers and hoots from the balcony. Then bang, the doors flew open, the kids outside came rushing in.

"Geronimo," they shouted out.

The usual flashlight shining in faces, but no collars. Then it quieted down. After a few moments Becky leaned over and whispered in my ear.

"Do you want to go upstairs?"

"What?" I asked.

"I said, do.. you.. want.. to.. go.. upstairs?" she said louder.

"Shh", we heard from the Jewish kids around us.

Not sure what she had in mind, but it sounded intriguing.

"Okay, sure, let's go," I said.

"Excuse me, pardon, sorry, her idea, sorry. Her idea," I said as we squeezed out of our row.

We headed upstairs, Becky tugging my arm, leading the way. It was dark, some of the wall lights had been removed, for atmosphere. Becky lead me to a couple of seats in the far-right corner of the back row. We squeezed in; the kids were busy making out, so they weren't very accommodating.

"Excuse us, pardon, sorry, her idea, sorry. Her idea." And we settled in.

We were way up. I almost hit my head on the ceiling overhanging the balcony. Guess the rules for head room didn't exist in those days. I'm sitting there and I could hardly make out the screen much less hear the words. No wonder the Italian kids made out. Nothing else to do. And making out was what they were doing. Madonna mia. Practically my whole 9-14 class was there. Sal Glorioso was with Adele Monaco, boy I used to dream about her, and Vinny Caravella, was with Cookie Tomasulo, who I used to dream about, too. Sometimes they'd show up in the same dream.

All in all, there was a lot of huffing and puffing going on up there. If this was how you got into college, they'd all be going to Harvard. I was a nervous wreck. Mr. Big Shot, a chicken. I almost clucked myself, "Cluck, cluck, cluck, cluck. This was what I always wanted, Becky and me doing what the Italian kids did. Be careful what you wish for. Right?

Then suddenly Becky reached over and put my arm around her shoulder. She must've gotten tired waiting for me to make the first move. What first move? I was trying to watch the movie. I loved movies. I tried to make conversation.

"Good movie, so far," I said to Becky.

"Shh," from Sal Glorioso. I made a mental note, next time he tried to cheat off me, I'd cover my paper.

We sat there for what seemed like an eternity. It might have been. My arm fell asleep. Christ. What next? Shit, I had to pee. I took my arm gently off Becky's shoulder and whispered in her ear: "I have to go to the bathroom."

"Now? Can't you hold it?" she asked.

"No, I can't. It's a family weakness. I won't be long."

I got up and had to squeeze by everybody again. By now they wanted to kill me. But they knew they needed me to be promoted to high school, so they let me pass.

I entered the boy's bathroom and Johnny Parisi and Nancy Ruvolo were in a stall and they were 'doing it.' What's wrong with these people, I thought, can't they find a good Garofalo mattress somewhere, how's a guy going to concentrate? I went to a urinal as far away from the gyrating couple as possible.

I heard, "You're the best, Johnny. You're the best." An ego boost for Johnny for sure but I had to get out of there. Thank God I was able to pee. A quick wash up and I was out the door. I walked along the carpeted area behind the backrow seats, so I didn't have to disturb anyone. I hopped over the back of my seat and settled in.

"Miss me?" I said.

Was I cool or what?

"I did. I almost came after you," she cooed.

"What did I miss?" referring to the flick.

"This!" She said.

Becky gave me a French kiss. Not the American version of the French kiss, but the way the French must do it. They must do it good to have it named after them. I thought, I always liked the French. French kiss, French fries, French pastry, Maurice Chevalier, Brigitte Bardot, no wonder they didn't like anybody. They're superior to the rest of us. We kissed for the rest of the movie. I think our lips were black and blue at the end.

After the movie, I walked Becky home. It was a little awkward, usually we talked about the movie afterwards. What was your favorite part, how'd you like the writing, the acting? That sort of thing. But we couldn't do that because we hadn't seen the movie. I was good at dissecting a movie, Becky valued my analysis, she waited for it. But not that day. I dropped Becky off at The Le Parc building entrance. We didn't say much. Didn't have to. It had all been said. Done. Becky gave me a sweet peck on the cheek, and I noticed a red mark on her neck. A hickey. I had given Becky a hickey. I had marked her for the world to see. This was my woman, hands off. I had reached second base. I was very proud of myself. I waited for her to go inside.

I practically skipped home. I wondered if fifteen was too young to get married. I heard in parts of Africa they married young. National Geographic had an article on Pygmies. They married very young. I thought if two consenting pigmies could do it why not me and Becky.

The next day I woke up and decided to ask Becky to marry me that very day. Only I couldn't, it was Sunday and I had to be home for Sunday dinner. Uncle Sal and Bernice came in. The usual suspects were there. For some reason all the talk was about me.

"Suspended? He used to be such a good boy, what happened?" Uncle Sal asked.

"Too much with the television," my grandparents said.

"I don't blame the television, it's the school, they don't teach the kids to get along," Aunt Theresa said.

They talked amongst themselves as if I wasn't there.

"Helloo, I'm right here," I said.

The more I protested the more they ignored me.

"What is he going to do with his life?" Uncle Sal wanted to know. "He keeps changing his mind about a career. First, he wants to be a writer. Then he wants to go into construction. Which is it?" he asked.

"I don't know what to do with him anymore," my mother said.

"What about military school?" Aunt Jenny wondered.

"No. No military school," my father barked.

"Helloo, I'm right here," I said again.

"Maybe he's like his cousin Lenny, the troublemaker," Uncle Sal said. Uh oh.

The last thing you wanted was to be compared with cousin Lenny. He was doing time in California for armed robbery. The story goes he was transporting a U-Haul truck load of marijuana from Mexico to Fresno. When he got to Fresno, he backed into a gas pump while he was getting gas. You know, to leave the tank full, like when he got it. He was a crook, but a frugal one. Anyway, the truck burst into flames sending a huge marijuana mushroom cloud over all of Fresno. The judge asked him whether he was sorry for what he did.

"What are you talking about, it was the best thing that ever happened to Fresno," Lenny said.

That was Lenny, he couldn't help being a wise guy. Even if it cost him. He called me 'Stiff' because I was a good kid who obeyed the law. As if that was the bigger crime. Once when he was visiting, me and Howie were bemoaning the fact we had no money. Lenny suggested we knock over a store. Now why didn't we think of that? Obviously, he didn't know his audience.

But being set up by Charlie Giambo hardly qualifies as a budding criminal. I made my case at the table.

"You don't understand, Charlie took the pocketknife that Grandpa gave me for my birthday. I was just trying to get it back," I explained.

"Oh, that changes everything. A birthday present. I never did like that Giambo family. A bunch of cidrules if you ask me," Uncle Sal said.

Everyone at the table agreed. All cidrules. Every last one of them. I continued to make my case and by the time the cannolis came out everyone was ready to march on Seth Low Jr. High School and demand they let me back in.

I decided I better get my term paper done; time was running out. As I was working on it in the office Aunt Jenny pulled out her compact and started to powder her nose. Then I noticed she was a lot more dolled up than usual. Make-up, her hair was in a nice 'do', fingernails painted a bright purple. Her lips had bright red lipstick on. Bright, bright red lipstick, so bright that the light shining off it created a glare. She even had a little on her teeth. I felt an obligation to point it out. I didn't know much about lipstick. Becky didn't wear any, anti-woman, she said, but I knew having some on your teeth was not the look you were after. I smiled and pointed to my teeth. My aunt got it; she quickly wiped the lipstick off her teeth.

"How's that?" she asked me.

"Good," I said.

She looked in the mirror, pleased at the visage she saw. Then I took a wild guess. A wild, wild guess.

"Aunt Jenny, are you going out on a date?" I asked.

She closed the compact and without getting up, rolled over to me in her chair. Like that old Amish guy did in the movie 'Witness'. She looked around to make sure the coast was clear, and she said the three words we were all hoping to hear one day.

"I met someone." she said.

"Get out of here," I said.

"No, I'm serious," she said.

"Gee that's great, Aunt Jenny."

"What's his name?" I asked.

"Rudy Klecko," she said.

"Italian?" I asked.

"No. Czech," she answered.

"Catholic?" I asked.

"No. Jehovah's Witness," she said.

"Jehovah's Witness? Uh oh, better not tell Grandpa," I reminded her.

"Don't worry, I won't," she said.

"Does anyone else know about Rudy?" I asked.

"No, I was waiting to see how things developed before I brought him around," she said.

"What does he do?" I asked.

"He's inherited a business from his father. They're based in Staten Island. Klecko Cement. But I think he has potential elsewhere," she said.

She took out a photo from her blouse pocket and showed me.

"He's not your prince charming or anything but he's a good guy, he laughs at my jokes and he says he loves me," she said.

"Do you love him?" I asked.

"I'm not sure what love is, Joey. But I enjoy being with him. I think about him when he's not with me," she said.

"Sounds like love to me," I said.

Now I needed to ask a mature question.

"Are you going to get married?" I asked.

She thought about how to answer.

"He hasn't asked me yet, but I think it's coming," she said. "My whole life I've been living for other people. It's my turn now, Joe, my turn."

Chapter 6

Coming of Age

Jewish Community House

I decided to go to school to hand in my term paper. I went to the teacher's lounge and handed it to Mrs. Scalise. She read it right away. Then handed it back to me.

"It's good, but you need to go deeper," she said. "It lacks emotion."

Oh. Okay. I'll work on it some more. Emotion, huh? I was hoping for a better reaction, but deep down I knew it wasn't great. I needed more from my father. I took the paper, folded it in my back pocket, thanked Mrs. Scalise and left.

While I was at school, I figured I'd see Howie. He usually ate lunch across the street in Seth Low Park where the old guys came every day to play chess. Howie was playing that day. He played well. Bobby Fischer was his idol. Fischer grew up in Brooklyn, was Jewish, and was scary brilliant. Howie knew all of Fischer's openings and he'd try them out in the park. Fischer had beaten Ratmir Cholmov in Havana, Cuba and Howie was anxious to try the opening he used in the match. It was working because when I arrived, his opponent, old man Mendelson had only a King and a few pawns left. Howie was moving in for the kill. Howie nodded to me, put his hand up indicating for me to wait. Won't be long. I hung out and watched. Chess didn't hold a fascination for me. I knew how to play, but I needed a ball involved to get my attention. But I didn't mind watching. I liked the drama of it.

"Your move," Howie said as he looked at me as if to say, "Mr. Old Guy doesn't have a chance."

My mind began to wander. Why had Howie told Becky about Debbie Drake? I couldn't for the life of me figure out why. Then Howie moved his rook and it was curtains. Or as they say in Brooklyn, coitains.

"Checkmate," Howie declared.

Then he extended his hand with a big shit-eating grin on his face and old man Mendelson just walked away.

"Sore loser," Howie said to me.

It was getting late, so I walked Howie over to the school across the street. We passed the 'ghees' horsing around, chasing each other, hitting, laughing, not a care in the world. Being late to school didn't seem to faze them. Some of them didn't even go to school. But they hung out there anyway. Some Jewish kids made fun of them behind their backs. 'Dumb Italians,' they'd say. I got my feelings hurt. I was one of them. It wasn't that I was ashamed of being Italian. It was more like I lived in two worlds. At home in neither. But I compartmentalized my feelings. I let things go. When I felt bad for my Italian classmates, I thought these are the guys who were going to become carpenters, plumbers, electricians, drywallers and painters, and get even with everybody. Jews included. They'll show up late, if at all, never call, charge a lot, they'll have the last laugh. Funny how things balance out. God does work in mysterious ways.

I walked Howie to his homeroom class 9-1, where the Brainiac's were.

"Why'd you tell Becky about Debbie Drake?" I asked.

"Because I'm your best friend and best friends have each other's back," he answered.

I agreed but why did he feel he had to have my back.

"We're on the roof of the 'J'. Becky and I are helping out planning the dance next week and that no count Sidney Fishman asks her if she wants to go to the dance with him," Howie said.

"Sidney Fishman, the all-time schmuck, Sidney Fishman, the we hate his guts, Sidney Fishman?" I asked.

"One in the same," Howie said.

"Well, what'd she say?" I asked.

"No, of course. She was going with you. But he kept pursuing her, saying there was no future with you, you being a goy and all, no offense. I had to think quick. Make her jealous. All I could come up with was Debbie Drake. If a hot babe like her liked you she should appreciate what she had."

"You told her Debbie Drake was interested in me?" I asked Howie

"Yup," he said.

"She believed you?" I asked.

"Apparently. I heard from one Sal Glorioso that a certain somebody was upstairs with a certain somebody else." he said.

"Maybe."

"Maybe? Either you were upstairs, or you weren't? It's like being pregnant, either you are, or you aren't," he said.

"Okay, I was upstairs, but I wanted to be the one who told you not big mouth Sal Glorioso," I said.

"You owe me my friend. Because of me you went upstairs with Becky Fishbein," Howie declared.

"Thanks, Howie, I owe you," I said.

"Don't mention it. What are best friends for," he reminded me.

We arrived at class 9-1. It had been the first time I had seen the inside of this classroom. I saw kids with slide rules in their pockets, others were reading, doing homework, sharing math problems on the board. Problems even Einstein couldn't figure out. A big difference from what I was used to. Suddenly 9-14 was looking a lot better. Safer. Becky saw me and came over.

"Hi handsome," she said. "What brings you to this neck of the woods, slumming?"

Before I was able to come up with a witty reply a Brainiac came running in screaming at the top of his lungs:

"The baldies are coming! The baldies are coming!"

The girls started screaming, running in circles.

"The baldies are coming! The baldies are coming!" they yelled.

The baldies? Here? At Seth Low Jr. High School? In Brooklyn? How could that be? The Brainiac's weren't about to try to figure this one out they ran out of the classroom and into the street. Howie, Becky and I ran outside, too. We had heard of the baldies. They were a gang from the Bronx. They were also called the Fordham baldies. Rumor had it that they would go to schools and grab girls at random and cut off their hair. Hence the name baldies. But I thought they confined their barbering to the Bronx. The school was in a total panic. The teachers came outside and tried to play it down, but you could see they were in a panic, too. Especially the female teachers. The longer their hair the more terror on their face. Howie was sure it was a hoax. Becky and I weren't so sure. Big shot Howie decided to go home. No way would there be classes today. Becky couldn't go home; they were putting in wall to wall carpeting throughout her house, so she had to hang around. I decided we'd hide out under the football bleachers, just in case. We waited. And waited and waited. Becky was really scared. She was trying to use logic.

"They have to be real; things just don't come from thin air."

"But has anyone actually seen a baldie?" I asked.

"Sure. I guess. I don't know," she said.

"Any pictures?" I asked.

"I don't know that either. But they are supposed to have leather jackets and tattoos all over their bodies," she said.

Becky admitted she was scared, and she cuddled up in my arms. I could see she expected me to assume my role as protector. I was up to the challenge. I removed my belt from my pants and wound it around my hand as if to say, "Don't come near my woman, Mister Baldie, or you'll get some of this."

I started strutting around like a peacock. Signifying. Daring them to show up. Becky started to laugh.

"You're funny."

"Yeah, funny on the outside, but a tiger on the inside. Roarrr."

Now she was really laughing. I started laughing, too. We're now laughing together. It was the kind of laughing that usually happened between two male friends. Howie and I had many such moments, but this was the first time I laughed like this with a girl. Unbridled, fall on the floor hysterics. I didn't think it was possible, but we certainly did it. It lasted a full five minutes. At least. It was only because our stomachs hurt that we stopped. After we composed ourselves, we huddled together some more. It was getting cold; winter was around the corner. I took off my sweater and wrapped it around Becky. Something Sidney Fishman in his wildest dreams would never think of, that selfish S.O.B. I was building up a real distaste for the guy.

We waited. One o'clock. No sign of the baldies. Two o'clock. No baldies. Three o'clock. Nope, not a one. By then it was time to go home. I walked Becky home. She called me her protector. She gave me back my sweater, gave me a sweet kiss on the cheek and went inside her building. We never found out if the baldies really existed or not. Maybe it was somebody's idea of a bad joke. But for that day I got to play Joey, the Protector, and I liked it.

A few days later I was at the construction yard. My grandfather had me cleaning the big equipment. Top to bottom. Had my cloth rag, some solvent and I was rubbing the metal, getting it spotless. Little did I know I was getting it spotless for Jimmy Giambo. A month had passed, and my grandfather hadn't paid his bill. At exactly noon time, Jimmy showed up with his brother, Mike the cop from the 62nd precinct to get his backhoe. They are in Mike the cop's police car. Mike the cop, that's how he was known in the neighborhood. You couldn't say Mike without adding 'the cop.' It was because it was a miracle this guy was on the right side of the law and they needed to keep reminding themselves. He used to be Mike the hoodlum, Mike the JD, Mike the no count. Now he was Mike the cop.

That's the way it played out in the neighborhood. The hoodlums became cops. They stole hubcaps, cut school, sneaked in movies, shoplifted, but when it came time to pick a career, they chose cop. When they became cops most of them were power hungry, wanting to get even for perceived slights they felt growing up.

That day Mike the cop did the talking saying if my grandfather refused to give back the backhoe, he would be forced to arrest him. He was bluffing but my grandfather knew he had no right to hold on to something he couldn't pay for. He had to let it go. The men lined up to see the backhoe being driven up on to a big flatbed trailer. Then Jimmy motioned the trailer driver to head out. Then he hopped in the police car with Mike the cop and they drove off. Mike the cop had his lights flashing. That was good, because the Palumbos didn't feel bad enough they needed flashing lights to advertise they couldn't pay their bills. The men didn't say a word, just shook their heads and went back to what they were doing.

My grandfather, father and I watched the whole thing from the office. It was too unbearable, a watershed moment for Palumbo & Sons. The beginning of the end.

The silver lining in it all was Jimmy Giambo had decided to move his operation to Staten Island and that meant he was going to take Charlie with him. That's when I learned nothing is all bad. My life would be immeasurably better with Charlie gone.

After that day some of the men began leaving the company. Some got jobs at other construction companies in Brooklyn, others moved to Staten Island to find work there. Ernie stayed, of course, and a few others. We started taking on small jobs. Repair work. No job too small. Painting a room, banging out a fence, replacing a door. It would be like if Itzhak Perlman couldn't get work at Carnegie Hall and he came to the Seth Low cafeteria to play his violin for the 9-14 table. Ernie handled everything. Thank God for Ernie, he kept us afloat.

My grandfather spent more time in the backyard and my father decided if we were ever going to remodel our tiny bathroom now was the time. Plus, with me not going to school I could be his helper. I liked that. Hands on experience. What better way to learn construction than from a master? As the saying goes, if you're given lemons make lemonade. And that's what we did. First, we had to get me set up. I got a pair of steel toed shoes. Then a carpenter's belt, tape measure, square, pencil, work gloves. What I didn't have my father had. We would share. First was the demo. Take everything out, sink, toilet, tub it all had to go.

"Get down to the studs," my father said.

"What's a stud?" I deadpanned.

"What?" he panicked.

"Gotcha, that's two," I said and hit my father twice in the arm.

I saw beaucoup trips in my future schlepping debris down the steep stairs and then right back up for another load.

"Don't worry, Joe, I got a better idea," he said.

That's the way the whole job went, I would think we had to do something one way and my father would come up with a better way. So instead of using the stairs we made a chute, we slid the debris down two floors instead of carrying it down. Brilliant.

My mother helped pick out a new light fixture, a fancy dancy sink, some wallpaper. A European toilet that hung on the wall so you could easily clean under it. Spiffy. Even though she had her heart set on moving to Staten Island she made a deal with my father, if he agreed to go to therapy for his anger issues she would help with the decorating.

Meanwhile she was doing quite well in "The Real Estate." Opening escrows, closing escrows. I didn't understand what an escrow was, but I knew it was followed by a check. During the construction we had to use Aunt Theresa's bathroom. I didn't realize how much she watched soap operas. "General Hospital," "As the World Turns," "One Life to Live," she went from one to the other. And she would talk to the television.

"Watch out behind you." "Don't believe her, she's the one who killed him."

Occasionally I took a break and sat with her and watched. Her face would light up. I couldn't believe how so little a thing could bring that much pleasure to someone. She would tell me the back story, what I'd missed. She would bring out watermelon. She cut it in little squares and sprinkled it with salt. She once called me Eddie, her dead husband, by mistake.

I learned a lot that month from my father. It seemed therapeutic for him. We did everything, carpentry, plumbing, electrical, sheet rocking, painting, the whole shebang. No subs on this job. Working with my father was a treat. But the most fun part was the lunches. My grandmother made us lunch every day. We'd talk. About everything. I would ask questions and my father would do his best to answer them. We got personal.

"Do you ever wish you had done something else with your life?" I asked him.

"No, not really," he answered.

"C'mon, Dad. You can tell me," I insisted.

"You'll laugh," he said.

"No, I won't, tell me," I said.

"I always wanted to be a dancer. Like Fred Astaire," he said.

I couldn't hold back. I cracked up.

"See, I told you," he said.

We both started to laugh. Then it got serious. I saw my opening. The deadline for my term paper loomed.

"What happened over there, Dad? What happened that you don't want to talk about?" I asked.

"You don't want to know," he said.

"I do. I need to know," I said.

My father could see I really wanted to know. He closed his eyes going back to that day that he'd pushed back in his memory. That box he was afraid to open. Then it all flowed out:

"We were walking through the jungle looking for Charley. About ten of us. We were moving quietly with sixty-pound backpacks and rifles ready to shoot. It was hot, we were soaked to the bones. And dark. Pitch black. Then suddenly out of the trees came about twenty Vietcong, with spears, knives, anything they

164

could get their hands on. My buddies began falling to the ground. We panicked. We started firing. Now the Vietcong are going down. It's bedlam. My gun jams, and this Vietcong sees his opportunity and he comes at me, slashing away. I grab the knife away from him, a pocketknife - and I plunge it into his stomach. And again. It was a knife like your grandfather gave you. The kind he said that couldn't hurt anybody."

Then he opened his eyes and looked at me, tears streaming down his face.

"I bent down and I turned him over. He was a kid, Joey. It could've been you."

I didn't know what to do. I had no experience comforting grown-ups much less my father. I thought of Becky, she'd know what to say. Even Howie was pretty good. Then the words just came out:

"It wasn't your fault, Dad. It wasn't your fault."

My father nodded. He knew it deep down, but it was nice to hear it out loud.

I immediately ran to the school library and started working on the term paper. From scratch. I must've gotten the emotion of the story, I cried like a baby writing it. It felt good to complete it. It had been weighing on me.

With the term paper and remodel done I suddenly had time to kill. My Aunt Essie had been wanting me to trim her hedges, so I figured this was as good a time as any. Aunt Essie was the saint of the family. Our very own Mother Theresa. God bless this, God Bless that, with God's help, you get the picture. She was almost totally deaf now and she refused to get a hearing aid. She was married to another Uncle Joe, the violin playing Joe not the bedding Joe. Uncle Joe was a professional musician. He also played base, guitar, the mandolin. Anything with strings. The problem was he never got out of his pajamas anymore. He had become a recluse.

I went over there, and my aunt gave me the hedge clippers.

"Thanks," I said.

"What??" she asked.

"THANKS!" I said louder.

"What?" she asked again.

"He said thanks," Uncle Joe called out.

"Oh, I thought he said tanks. Like in the army."

Somehow, she heard him. They communicated like dolphins with the beeps and echoes of their sonar.

It was hard being around my aunt. You couldn't have a normal conversation with her. But somehow my uncle could. They had a real, deep love between them. And they couldn't be more appreciative over the littlest things you did for them.

"Look Essie what a nice job he did," he said.

"Incredible, what an eye he has, God bless him," she said.

"This boy is going places. There is something special about this boy. I'm not sure what it is but I know he's going to bring honor to the family," Uncle Joe boasted.

"With the grace of God, he will," Aunt Essie agreed.

All this praise was making me uncomfortable. I wanted to go home. But Uncle Joe wanted to talk, man to boy.

"Sit for a little while. Essie, give Joey the Yankee Doodles we got for him for doing the hedges," he said.

My aunt headed for the cupboard.

"Maybe a few minutes," I said.

"So, what's new, Joey? How are things going with your girlfriend, Bonnie?

"Becky," I corrected him.

"Yes, of course, Becky, such a pretty name," he said.

Then he got two inches from my face. Uh oh. Here it comes.

"Are you using protection?" he whispered.

167

"You mean?.."

"You know," he whispered.

I didn't know why we were whispering. Aunt Essie couldn't hear a word.

"Well actually I'm only at second base," I confided.

"That's good. There's plenty of time for the other bases after you're married," he advised. "Your aunt and I don't play baseball anymore."

Yikes! I needed to get off the subject.

"This Saturday night, I'm taking Becky to a dance at the 'JCH' on the roof," I said.

"Really? I played there once. A bar mitzvah. It was wonderful," he said.

Then he started to sing Hava Nagila and stamp his feet to the tune. I thought to myself, this guy is very lively for a recluse.

"Are you a good dancer, Joe?" he asked.

"Not really," I admitted.

"Oh, come on, you're Italian, you have music in your soul. Come I'll show you," he offered.

In his pajamas he took my hands in his and started teaching me how to dance. The fox trot... One two three, four, one two three four. Then he put on a record and started showing me how simple it was to dance the Lindy.

"He's wonderful, Essie. Look. A girl can't resist a man who's a good dancer, right Essie?" he asked.

"What?" she asked from the bathroom.

"Never mind, sweetheart." He turned to me and said, "You gotta love her."

I headed home and decided that's what I wanted in my life. Forget about a career, I wanted what Uncle Joe and Aunt Essie had. Unconditional love. When I arrived home, my neighbor Mr. Ozeri was waiting for me. He needed my help. I was the Shabbos Goy for the Syrian Jews. A Shabbos Goy is a non-Jew who performs certain types of work which religious law prohibits a Jew to do on the Sabbath. Like turning on lights or driving a car. Mr. Ozeri wanted me to turn on the television. Technically I heard this was frowned upon by the rabbis. But I did it for him anyway. He was an old guy who lived alone. I felt sorry for him. Besides I figured he's the one going to burn in hell, not me.

Saturday night rolled around. I got a corsage for Becky and picked her up. We met outside The Le Parc. I pinned the corsage on her using the light from a lamppost to see. She loved it. A good start for the evening.

It was a beautiful fall evening in Brooklyn. We could've taken a bus, the B6 stops in front of the 'J', but Becky wanted to walk. So, we walked. A happy wife is a happy life. Same applies to girlfriends. The trees were losing their leaves and it made a beautiful cover for the sidewalk. It was getting chilly now, the hint of winter in the air. A few snow flurries started to gently fall as Becky put her arm in mine and the world seemed right.

We got to the 'J' and Becky waved to the admitting clerk and he signaled for her to go in. I had to show my membership card. The man gave a good long look. He knew me as well as he knew that mole on his cheek, but every time he made me show my card. His look said: 'How did you this card'? It wasn't easy getting that card. At first, they refused to let me join. This was just before my father left for Vietnam. When I told my father what had happened he got upset.

"If I can defend our country you should be able to get in the 'J'," he said.

We marched over to the 'J', my father in his full uniform, and he asked to see the head director. Mr. Gould came out and asked what the problem was. My father told him what had happened. Mr. Gould seemed honestly ashamed of what transpired.

"And to the son of one of 'our boys'," he said.

Gould read the clerk the riot act and told him to sign me up. For free. The clerk reluctantly typed my name on a membership card and handed it over to me. Joseph Palumbo. Full Membership.

As soon as Becky and I walked inside we smelled the chlorine in the swimming pool. Potent. Unmistakable. We took the stairs and headed for the roof. The band was already playing. The stars were out that night, you could see the Milky Way, almost touch it. The band was playing a Beatles song. Everybody sang along and danced. We headed for the punch bowl. No alcohol, just a strawberry blend. We were sipping our drinks, the band started to play those distinctive beats of the Temptations hit 'My Girl'. Dum, dum, dum, dum, dum, dum, dum, dum, dum, and the crowd went crazy. I pulled Becky on the dance floor, the name, 'My Girl,' personified how I felt about her plus it was a slow dance, gave me a chance to snuggle up to her. Becky had her head nestled on my shoulder. I was holding her tight. I whispered in her ear, "Mi piaci tanto." She loved when I talked Italian. I loved when she talked Yiddish.

"Me, too, my little bubellah," she said. Speaking in foreign tongues added spice to our relationship. Things couldn't have been more perfect, until I felt a tap on my shoulder. I turned around and it was that no count Sidney Fishman.

"May I cut in?" Fishman asked.

Cut in? The nerve of this guy. Becky turned him down once, but some guys can't take a hint. Maybe he still hadn't gotten over the fact I stole the ball from him.

"Do you mind?" Fishman asked Becky sweetly.

"Just one dance, it'll be okay," Becky said to me.

That was the only thing I didn't like about Becky. She avoided confrontation at all costs. Becky went from my arms into the arms of Sidney Fishman. I was pissed.

I went over to the punch bowl and watched. Howie came over.

"I wouldn't let that go on too long," Howie said.

"Don't worry, I won't," I said.

Fishman could really dance. Gene Kelly dance. He brought her closer to him. Then he did a dip. Hey, I was going to do that. Uncle Joe showed me that move. Then he pulled Becky in real close, too close for my comfort. I slammed my drink down and walked over. I tapped Fishman on the shoulder. He ignored me. I tapped him again. Harder. Still nothing. I hit his shoulder now. Fishman turned to me.

"What do you want, Palumbo?" Fishman asked.

"It's my turn," I said.

Fishman scoffed, and turned back to Becky. They continued to dance. I hit him on the shoulder again.

"Maybe you didn't hear me, I said it's my turn," I said getting hot.

"Get lost, pizza man." Fishman barked.

As Popeye used to say: "I can't stands no more."

Bam. I hit him in the stomach. Fishman dropped to his knees, gasping for air.

"What'd you do that for?" Becky said to me.

She went over to help him.

"You know you have a real problem, Joey," Becky told me.

Hey, you have the wrong guy, I wanted to say. But I was so pissed, I just left.

I ran home. That was the last time I stepped foot in the 'J'. As far as I was concerned if I was looking for unconditional love it certainly wasn't coming from Becky.

Maybe it was time for me to move on. Get a nice Italian girl. But who? There were certainly some nice ones in my class. Adele. Connie. Marie. Yeah, Marie. I had her number. True, she sneaked it in my pocket when I wasn't looking, but she was a looker. I waited a few days and decided to give her a call.

"Hello?" I heard Marie say.

"Hi, this is Joey Palumbo," I said.

"Well, hi, Joey Palumbo," Marie answered.

"I was wondering if you want to..." I said.

"Yes, I do," she answered before I could complete my sentence.

"I heard you had a falling out with that Jewish girl. I figured you might be calling."

"Well, yeah, right, I did. I am," I said.

"Hey, listen, my parents are going out tonight. If you want to come over you can," she said.

"Sure. What time?" I asked.

"How about sevenish?" she said.

"Okay, seven it is," I said.

I went over to her house at seven. I rang the bell. Marie appeared at the door. She looked hot. Debbie Drake hot. She invited me in.

"Hi Marie. Nice...

Before I could finish, she was smothering me with kisses.

"Hold on, Marie, shouldn't we talk a little?"

"Okay, let's talk. Nice weather we're having," she joked.

Then she began to undo my shirt.

"What's the hurry?" I asked her.

"My parents will be home in an hour."

"I'm sorry, Marie, I don't perform well under pressure."

"What pressure?" she asked.

"You know, one hour before they'll be home pressure," I said.

"C'mon, stop kidding around," she said getting impatient.

"You know I just realized something. I have to rewrite a term paper that's due. I'm sorry. I'll call you. We'll do this another time. Soon. I promise," I said.

I ran out of there, dressing as I went. Marie just stood at the door.

I realized I might have to wait awhile before I jumped back into the dating scene. I needed time to get over Becky. I knew after that one night with Marie it wasn't going to be so easy.

My sixteenth birthday fell on a Sunday. My grandmother made capuzzelle in my honor. The usual suspects were there plus we had a new face at the table. Howie. Yup the first Jew to have Sunday dinner with us. Capuzzelle is the most tender meat you'll ever have, if you can get past how it looks. A lamb's head on a platter seems more reminiscent of a scene from a horror movie. Pointy ears, big snout, bulging eyes, even the teeth were cooked and on display. Everyone cheered when my grandmother brought it out. Howie almost plotzed.

"You want the eyes?" Uncle Frankie teased Howie.

"That's okay, I had eyes for breakfast," Howie quipped, aghast that people would even consider eating the eyes of this poor lamb.

I was confident that Howie's sense of humor would get him through the meal. But I did have doubts about what my family might say. It's not that they didn't like Jews, they just really didn't know any.

"I can tell by the look on your face you've never killed anybody," Uncle Sal asked Howie.

"Killed anybody? I never even pushed anybody," Howie kidded back.

Uncle Sal let out a big laugh, hit Howie on the back.

"I like this kid, Joey." (to Howie) "Anybody give you trouble you come to me," Uncle Sal said offering his Mafia backing.

By then everyone received a portion of lamb and we began eating. Uncle Frankie and Uncle Tommy began to eat out of Howie's plate. A test to see if Howie could take a joke. It was okay with Howie, he wasn't going to touch this food anyway.

"So Joey tells us you want to be a doctor?" my father said.

"Yes, a pediatrician," Howie said. "I want to work with kids. I think I can be most helpful there."

"The world can always use a good doctor," my mother said.

"No, a great doctor," I said. "One time some boys were playing touch football in the park. Jimmy Lakiotis threw a long pass to Steven Singer who raced after it and BAM ran right into a metal pole. The pole shook as Singer layed on the ground in pain. Nobody knew what to do. Howie shows up.. "Joey, you call an ambulance." "Benny, roll up your jacket and make a pillow." "Gary, go get a blanket from one of the strollers." "Petie, get me a wet rag." All the while he's holding Singer's tongue so he doesn't choke. He was amazing."

Everyone agreed: "Wow." "Amazing."

"Thanks for the plug, Joe, I'll handle it from here. It was no big deal. I learned what to do in an emergency from my father," said Howie downplaying the event.

Meanwhile Howie had only poked at his food.

"The food's great, Mrs. Palumbo," he said, trying to change the subject off of him.

My grandmother smiled. She knew a non eater when she saw one.

"So what kind of food do 'you' people eat?" asked my grandfather.

"It's your people, Grandpa," I corrected him

"That's what I said," my grandfather said.

"No, you said 'you' people. I heard it," my mother said backing me up.

"That's not politically correct, Grandpa," I said.

"Pop, you shouldn't be even asking that," my father said.

"I'm just trying to get into the conversation. Jeesh," my grandfather said getting frustrated.

"That's okay, I got it. We eat gefilte fish, bagels, pastrami, you know JEW food," Howie quipped.

The people at the table cringed at the word 'Jew'.

"It's ok to say Jew. We don't take it as an insult. See..

(dangles a Star of David hanging from his neck).. says right here. Jew."

"Eddie had a Jewish friend. Jew friend. Seymour. He made hats. Ya-mul-kes," Aunt Theresa said.

"Yes, yamulkes, we don't leave home without them."

Howie took a yamulke out of his back pocket and waved it around.

"Why do you, your people perform circumcisions, if I can ask that question?" my grandfather wondered.

"Grandpa," I admonished him.

"Pop," my father said.

"He's going to be a pediatrician. I'm just letting him know what he'll have to do," my grandfather explained.

Howie put his hand up. He had it covered.

"We do it for sanitary reasons. In our schtetls in Poland, that's Yiddish for small towns, there was a lot of hay. In the barns. It got all over everything. So we started to circumcise the, you know, it cleaned things up," Howie answered.

"We don't do that in the Catholic religion," my grandfather stated.

"I know. To each his own I always say," said Howie.

Howie did a pretty good job defending 'his' people and their customs. However, when the cannolis came out it degenerated into a competition between Howie and my grandfather over whose religion was better. Yup, a 'faith off'.

"We have the Seven Sacraments," my grandfather offered.

"We have the Ten Commandments," Howie retorted.

"We have the New Testament," my grandfather said.

"We have the Old Testament," Howie answered.

"We have Christmas Day," said my grandfather.

"We have Hannukah. 8 days," Howie responded.

"We have Jesus," my grandfather declared.

"We have Moses," Howie responded.

"Jesus was the son of God," my grandfather bragged.

"Jesus was a Jew," Howie said topping him.

My grandfather stood up.

"The hell he was, the Jews made that up!" he said getting his dander up.

Howie stood up.

"Uh, you know I better go. I have to study for a big algebra test. That's another thing *us Jews* are good at. Algebra. Thanks so much Mrs. Palumbo for the best tasting meat I almost ate. Next time I might even try the eyes. Bye," said Howie as he headed out.

Howie passed by me and whispered in my ear:

"See you tonight, birthday boy."

Then he grabbed a cannoli to go and he never came back. Smart boy.

Howie was planning something special for me. I was the first of our group to reach sixteen and I was feeling good about that. My driver's license was just around the corner. The only hint Howie would give me was we'd be going to Manhattan. At night. That meant right away I couldn't tell anyone in my family. Manhattan by day was bad enough but by night it would be a disaster waiting to happen. On the scope of the Japanese bombing Pearl Harbor. I told my parents Howie was treating me to a local movie and then we'd go to Jahn's on 86th Street for ice cream sodas. They shouldn't wait up. They had no reason to doubt me.

I kissed my mom goodbye and walked to The Le Parc to pick up Howie.

"Hey birthday boy. Ready for your present?"

"I don't know, depends on what it is," I said.

"You'll find out soon enough. Come on, let's go. Our appointment is at 8PM, we don't want to be late."

"For what?" I asked trying to trick him.

"That's for me to know and for you to find out. Nana, nana, nana," he said.

We headed for the train station on Bay Parkway. Howie handed me a token and we went through the turnstile. We went to the Northern end for a change, Manhattan bound, the sign read. Down the stairs and on to the platform. We sat on a wooden slat bench that was missing a few slats. We waited. I glanced over at the third rail and fortunately I didn't have to pee. Howie nervously patted down his cowlick. It kept popping up. He spit in his hand and patted it down again. This time it stayed. Finally, the N train came with the destination MANHATTAN displayed. We got on board. It wasn't very crowded. It was Sunday night. We took our seats by the door. It only sat two, that was good, no weirdos to worry about. It was nine stops to Manhattan. We headed out. Eventually we crossed the Brooklyn Bridge and the train came to a stop. We heard 'Canal Street' over a loudspeaker and looked at each other. We were in Manhattan. Adventure couldn't be too far behind. So far so good. We hadn't been robbed or killed. Howie didn't have much to say. He just sat there with this shit eating grin on his face. We stayed on the train until we hit 42nd Street. Howie hit my leg, time to get off. Now I was thinking he was going to take me to one of the girlie shows, sneak in somehow. We started to exit.

"Not yet. This way," Howie said.

We got on another train heading north. I was beginning to get nervous because the passengers were starting to get noticeably browner. I was as liberal as the next guy, but I also knew I didn't want to go where I wasn't wanted. I already had a taste of that, and it didn't taste good. But I was game. If you wanted adventure you had to be adventurous.

"Okay, this is us," Howie said.

We got off at 125th street. Spanish Harlem. Puerto Rican territory. Okay, I was cool. I'd never actually met a Puerto Rican, but I'd seen them in movies. I loved West Side Story. The music? Fuhgeddaboudit. "I want to be in America, okay by me in America, everything free in Americaaa..."

We exited the train, walked up the stairs and headed outside. We immediately knew we stepped into a different world. Salsa music was blaring from loudspeakers, we passed little bodegas, and on every corner street vendors peddled shaved ice and syrup. I thought to myself these people brought the island with them. The streets were full of young people, hanging out, dancing to the pounding beat of the music. It was exciting, intoxicating. A lively bunch, these Puerto Ricans. And the girls, madonna mia, were they dressed provocatively. Much more so than Marie and the Italian girls in Seth Low Park. We got some strange looks, young men wondering what a couple of white boychiks were doing in their part of town. But we avoided eye contact, trying to keep at bay the NYC standard, "What are you looking at?" Two older men laughed as we walked by, one holding up his thumb and index finger about an inch apart, indicating something small.

"Don't mind them," Howie said.

How could I mind them, I didn't understand what they were laughing about? We walked a few more blocks and Howie stopped in front of a two-story brownstone. He looked at a piece of paper.

"This is it."

"This is what?" I asked.

"Your birthday present," he said. "Here's the deal. I go first, warm her up for you. Then you go. Got it?"

"No, I don't got it. What are we doing here?" I asked.

"This will be your first experience with a pro."

"What? A who-a?" I exclaimed.

"Don't be so Brooklyn. She's a beautiful woman performing a much-needed service. Happy birthday, best friend."

"Oh no, I'm not ready for this. I'll see you back home. If I make it back alive," I said.

I started to leave.

"Hey, you want to win Becky back, don't you?" he asked.

I stopped. "No. Yes. Maybe," I said.

"Look, you do. This will give you the confidence you need."

I walked back.

"What do you mean?" I asked.

"I heard what happened with Marie. This'll be your chance to redeem yourself."

"Who told you?" I asked him.

"Never mind who told me."

"What if I'm not ready to redeem myself," I said.

"Look you want to hit a home run, don't you?" he asked. "Of course, you do. Once you hit one it'll make it that much easier to hit another. I'm talking with Becky my friend," he said.

"What if Becky doesn't want to play home run derby with me?" sticking with the baseball metaphor.

"They all want to play home run derby, but you have to be ready to execute. Now come on," he said.

Howie practically dragged me up the concrete steps and we stopped at the door. He looked for a name on the directory. Rodriquez, N. He rang the bell.

"Ola?" a voice said.

"It's me, Howie. Howie Schwartz," he announced.

Bzzz. We went in. It was clean. As clean as my hallway. A fake potted ficus plant to the right of the door. Howie headed for an apartment door. I followed. Howie stopped, I bumped into him. We became Laurel and Hardy. Howie rang a bell. It didn't work. Then he knocked. Knock, knock, knock knock knock. A 'we're not the cops' knock. A few seconds went by. The door opened. Standing on the other side of the door was a rather sexy looking woman about thirty-five, not a wrinkle on her face, dressed provocatively, as you would expect, boobs spilling out of her blouse.

"Entrar, come," she said, in Spanglish, motioning us to enter.

Howie knew a little Spanish, his housekeeper was teaching him.

"Gracias," he said.

We went in. Nice place, nice stuff, business must be good.

"Who is Signor Howie?" she asked.

"I am," Howie answered.

"He is," I answered also.

"Cual es your edad?" she asked.

"Eighteen, we're both eighteen." Howie said.

"Diez y ocho?" she said in Spanish.

She looked us over. Her eyes said, "Yeah, right."

"Is your primero time?" she said in Spanglish.

"Si, yes," we said. Nilda smiled.

She pointed to a chair.

"You esperar and Howie venir comnigo with Nilda," she said.

She talked in the third person, it made me nervous. Howie gave me a little wave and he followed Nilda into the bedroom. I sat in the chair. I saw a stack of magazines on the table next to me. I thought of my dentist's office, Dr. Kramer. Only these magazines weren't Sports Illustrated or Time Magazine. These were all girlie magazines. Written in Spanish. I didn't know how to read Spanish, so I just looked at the pictures. And as they say, a picture is worth a thousand

Spanish words. The apartment was small. My chair was right by the door to Nilda's bedroom. I heard everything and from the sound of things Howie was getting his money's worth. It seemed like he was in there for an hour. It was probably shorter but not that much. Finally, the noise stopped. I was sweating now, worried about my turn coming up. A few minutes passed and Howie came out.

"She called me, 'Howie the Terrific'. Your turn, birthday boy."

Howie sat in the chair, exhausted. Oh great, I thought, how could I measure up to that. Maybe she said that to all her clients. Yeah, so they would come back. I went in. Nilda was washing her hands in the bathroom connected to the bedroom, a master suite she had. Again, I thought, business must be good. Maybe Palumbo & Son could find out her secret.

"Ponte comodo," she said.

Hmm, I wasn't sure what she was saying, but I guessed it had to do with my clothes. Do I take all my clothes off, hop in bed? No, that might be too presumptuous, I didn't want to give her the wrong idea. Wait, Joe, she's being paid. I decided to take off my outer garments and my shoes. I left on my shorts, tee shirt and socks. My feet got cold; I didn't want to offend Nilda. She came out and stood by the door. In a sexy pose like you see in the movies, a dark silhouette figure backlit with the bathroom light.

"Are you ready for Nilda?" she said in perfect English.

I surmised this is what she had learned to say in America. To brand herself.

Ready for Nilda? If I lived a thousand years, I'd never be ready for Nilda.

I squeaked out a "Yes." Followed by a deeper voice, "Yes." Next she lied down on the bed and motioned for me to lie down next to her. I did. She touched me. It must have been the magazines, in a second it was over. We both got dressed, no words were exchanged, and we exited the bedroom. Howie paid Nilda and gave her a tip. Fifteen percent. He always went by the rules. We left.

I couldn't tell Howie what had happened. Or rather what had not happened. As far as he was concerned it was the best birthday present a friend could ever receive.

Chapter 7

Saddle Up the Horses

Verrazano Bridge

That next Sunday dinner we had a visitor from Staten Island, Aunt Jenny's new boyfriend. I liked him right off. He was a good guy and he really liked my aunt. We were hanging out before dinner and Rudy was showering Aunt Jenny with compliments.

"Jenny is so smart, so kind, so funny," he said.

"Oh, go on," she said. After a beat. "I said go on."

He realized she was making a joke and he burst out laughing. I loved seeing my aunt so happy. She deserved it in spades. My grandfather was suspicious of Rudy. He didn't like the fact he wasn't Italian, or Catholic, but Rudy was smart, he knew if he could win over the women, the men would follow. Instead of bringing a few bottles of wine to dinner, he brought American Indian bracelets. He gave one to each of the women.

"Jenny you don't mind your boyfriend giving other women such expensive gifts?" Aunt Theresa teased.

"I'll take my chances," Aunt Jenny joked back.

The bracelets were a big hit. No, a huge hit. My grandmother put on hers right away and modeled it for my grandfather.

"Isn't this beautiful, Vince?"

"If you're an Indian," he said, not willing to budge an inch.

Aunt Jenny took control of the whole dinner. The cooking, the serving, the cleaning up. The women tried to help but weren't allowed. My grandmother had a hard time controlling herself.

"Let me help you with that," she kept saying.

"I got it, Ma, I got it. Just sit. Relax."

Finally, my grandmother sat back and gave in to taking one day off. And she thoroughly enjoyed it.

"Dinner's ready," Aunt Jenny announced. "Sit where you want," she said to Rudy. Wouldn't you know it, he sat in my grandfather's chair.

"That's my chair," my grandfather barked.

Rudy jumped out of the chair as if he had sat on a tack. Aunt Jenny patted a chair next to her.

"Over here, next to me," Jenny said.

Rudy sat down gingerly. Okay, no harm no foul. We all looked at the cuckoo clock and waited. Rudy knew enough not to say or do anything. The cuckoo struck two and my grandmother was about to say the prayer when Aunt Jenny jumped in.

"I got it, Ma."

"I could get used to this," my grandmother cooed.

We all bowed our heads. Rudy looked around then bowed his head. For the first time at Sunday dinner Aunt Jenny said the prayer.

"Bless us Oh Lord and these Thy gifts which we are about to receive from Thy bounty through Christ our Lord." And then she added, "And thank you for bringing Rudy to our table today. Amen."

Everyone joined in, "Amen."

"Maybe Rudy would like to do his prayer today," I suggested. I was determined to make Rudy feel welcome, the pangs of John Page still haunting me.

"We already said grace. The food will get cold," my grandfather said.

"Rudy, would you like to say grace?" my father asked.

Rudy looked at my grandfather, then Aunt Jenny. She motioned it was okay.

"Okay," he said.

Rudy extended both hands out, Jehovah's Witness style. Aunt Jenny took one hand and I took his other. Now everyone was holding hands. My father grabbed my grandfather's hand.

"Be a good sport," he said.

I found it weird holding a strange man's hand. Bad enough when I danced with Uncle Joe, but he's family, this was different. Rudy's hand was very smooth for a cement guy. Guess he had his workers do the physical work. Rudy cleared his throat.

"Thank you, God, for the food we have on our table and the friends and family we have to share it with. Please forgive us for our sins. Through Jesus' name. Amen."

Amens all around. Even my grandfather mumbled a reluctant Amen.

"I like your prayer better than ours," I said. "It's simpler, more heartfelt. Mind if we use it when you're not here?" I joked.

"Oh, no, use it as much as you like." Rudy said, feeling pretty good about himself.

We began to eat the antipasto. People were going a little overboard on compliments.

"This is so good, Jenny," my mother said.

"It's the best antipasto I ever had," Aunt Theresa chimed in.

"Definitely," Uncle Tommy said.

"Better than mine," my grandmother said.

"So tasty," my father said.

Aunt Jenny, always the truth teller, couldn't take it.

"Would you stop already, it's hard to screw up antipasto."

Everyone laughed as if she made the greatest joke of all time.

"What a sense of humor," my mother said.

"She could be on television," Aunt Theresa added.

"I give up," Aunt Jenny said.

The conversation was a little awkward that day. People didn't quite know how to behave. We weren't used to Aunt Jenny bringing someone home, so we just ate our food. Finally, I had to say something.

"You like meat, Rudy?"

"Yes, I do," Rudy responded, happy the ice was broken.

"Good, because we got a lot of meat, right Dad?"

"Right, Joe, a lot of meat," my father agreed.

We passed our plates to Aunt Jenny and she went into the kitchen to put them in the sink and get the next course. On the way out she signaled Rudy to say something to my grandfather. A plan had obviously been hatched to win him over.

"Vince, if I may call you Vince?"

My grandfather glared at him. Rudy recoiled a bit but charged on.

"Jenny tells me you like baseball. I like baseball. Joe DiMaggio was my favorite player."

"He was alright," my grandfather said.

"Alright? Grandpa, do you feel okay? Joe DiMaggio is your favorite player, too," I said.

"But really I'm a big Brooklyn Dodger fan. I hated when they moved to California," Rudy said.

My grandfather wasn't going to make this easy.

"Who cares about baseball anyway? It's a boring game," he said.

"Grandpa!" I said.

But before he could go on, Aunt Jenny came in with a big platter of macaroni. Rudy sprung out of his chair to help her put it on the table. All the men looked on in amazement. My grandfather wasn't too thrilled at this male first in this house.

"Pop, Rudy wants to start a new business. Maybe you could give him some pointers," Aunt Jenny said.

"Jen tells me you're one heck of a businessman," Rudy said.

"What kind of business?" my grandfather asked.

"Selling American Indian jewelry. In New Mexico," Rudy said.

"New Mexico? I thought you were in the cement business in Staten Island," my grandfather responded.

"I am. But Jenny has this crazy notion maybe I could turn my interest in Indian jewelry into a business," Rudy said.

"It takes money to start a business," my grandfather said.

"Rudy has the money. His cement business is doing great," Aunt Jenny said. "Uncle Sal uses him all the time."

"Well, really it was my father's business. He's the one who built it up. I just took over after he passed away," Rudy admitted.

"Rudy wants to start something on his own," Aunt Jenny added, "do his own thing, as the kids say now."

"And Jenny would help. She's great with numbers. Much better than me. We would be partners. Equal partners."

Who is this guy, I wondered? I wanted to marry him. If Jehovah's Witnesses were all this sweet, I might have to join the flock.

Then my grandfather looked directly at my father as he spoke.

"It's easy to move away, start something new. What's hard is to stay home, stick to something that people have put their whole lives into building. A business that people depend on to keep going in good times and bad."

"Well, I think Rudy should go for it," my father said.

"Me, too," said my mother.

"Me, too," said Uncle Tommy.

"Me, too. And I'm sure if Eddie were here, he would think so, too," Aunt Theresa said emphatically.

They were obviously going around the table now. Eyes on my grandmother, still admiring her bracelet.

"Me, too," she said.

Uh oh, my turn. Everyone looked at me. The pressure was on, I had to give an answer.

"Me, too," I said.

My grandfather was crushed. Et Tu, Brute? Caesar was alone now, and he knew it.

"I think he should stay home and stick to what he knows. CEMENT!" he declared.

The ninety-pound sack had just been dropped on Rudy and his dream. Aunt Jenny lost it. She threw down her napkin and ran off crying. Rudy ran after her. My father got up, threw down his napkin.

"Suddenly I'm not hungry," he said.

He left the table.

"Me, neither," my mother said.

She left the table. Aunt Theresa and Uncle Tommy left also. That left me and my grandparents. Suddenly, unexpectantly my grandmother got up and left. That left me and my grandfather alone at the table. I was in this position once before, but I was sixteen now, and the main thing - I wasn't about to reward bad behavior.

"Me, neither," I said.

I left the table.

I went upstairs. By then my father and mother were in a tense discussion. I stood by the door in the hallway. I didn't want to intrude.

"That's the last straw. I've had it," my father said.

"Danny, please, he'll hear you."

"Let him hear me. After all Jenny's done for this family this is how he acts. I wouldn't blame her if she never speaks to him again," he said.

"He's under a lot of pressure, Dan, the business is on its last legs and he knows it. Cut him some slack."

"He was talking to me, Gina. That stuff about sticking it out and having people depend on you. And poor Rudy caught in the middle. You know what the problem is, Gina?"

"What?" she asked.

"We live here waiting for something to happen. Well, it's not going to happen unless we make it happen. We need our own place, Gina."

That night I couldn't sleep. What was the point of doing all this remodeling if we were going to move?

Leaving Brooklyn? My family? Howie? My school? Seth Low Park? Becky, even though she hated me. I wouldn't go. Simple, case closed. I'll stay with my grandparents. They'd be happy to have me. After Aunt Jenny marries Rudy, I can have her bedroom. Then when I turn eighteen my grandfather will bring me into the business, if there is one, and then I'll get my own place. Bada Bing, what's so hard? On the other hand, I was intrigued by Staten Island. Wide open spaces, a pool, big grassy lawns. I thought of Ebbetts field. I could have Ebbetts field as my back yard. And my mother really wanted to go. I hated to disappoint her. I'd have to think some more. Run it up the flagpole. In the meantime, I was hungry. I hadn't finished my meal. I went downstairs to raid the refrigerator. I overheard my grandparents in their bedroom.

"We're too close. We're getting on each other's nerves," my grandmother said.

"We're fine," my grandfather said.

"Maybe this is a good time to get away. Take a vacation."

"We don't need a vacation."

"It'll be good for us. We haven't done anything fun since I don't know when. Come on, what do you say, it'll take your mind off the business?"

"We don't have the money," he said.

"Yes, we do. I still have the money from when Papa died. We can use that."

"Maybe. Later," he said.

"Later, when? When we're in walkers? Or in the grave? I'm tired, Vince. Tired of cooking and cleaning every day. I need a break."

Silence.

"You're an old stubborn mule, that's what you are. An old stubborn mule," my grandmother said.

The next day my one-month suspension was up. I walked to school with Howie.

I wasn't ready to tell him we were moving, I wanted to be farther along, people change their minds, why get him all upset. I ran something else by him, something I thought about all night.

"If somebody is nice to you, but not nice to other people, can you still love that person?" I asked.

"Depends," he said.

"On what?" I asked.

"On how nice he is to you and how mean he is to other people. Hitler was nice to his dog but if the dog knew how mean he was to other people he would have bitten him," Howie said.

"Well he's very nice to me," I said

"Who're we talking about, Joe?" asked Howie.

"My grandfather. He was very mean to my aunt's boyfriend at dinner yesterday," I said.

"The JW?" he asked.

"Yeah, him," I answered.

"Look, Joey, your grandfather's going through some difficult times. He took it out on the JW. But you can still love him."

"That's good, because I do still love him. A lot," I said.

Howie was no Becky, but he was insightful, for a guy. We walked on a few steps more and it came out. It just came out.

"I think we're going to move," I said.

Howie stopped in his tracks.

"What?" he asked.

"At least my folks are talking about it," I added.

"Where?" he asked.

"To Staten Island," I said.

"When?" he asked.

"As soon as my mom finds a house. But not long," I said.

"What a revolting development this is," he said, uttering the line from the Great Gildersleeve TV show.

"I don't really want to move but I guess I have to," I said.

"I'm going to miss you, best friend," Howie said.

"I'll miss you, too. But I'll come around, I'll still come in for Sunday dinners. And holidays. Summers," I said.

"That's what Mike Pollack said when he moved to Long Island. But he never came back. Not once. Remember?" Howie said.

"Yeah, but that was Mike Pollack. I'll come back. I promise. You can come visit me, too. We'll be only an hour away, over the Verrazano Bridge. You can come swim in our pool," I said.

"Yeah, sure. That'll be great," he said.

We arrived at our usual breaking off place. Howie grabbed my arm so I couldn't go.

"One thing, I hate goodbyes. If it's okay let's say goodbye now," he said.

That seemed like an odd request but what the heck, if it made it less traumatic for him, I was willing to do it.

We hugged. We had never hugged before. This was before hugging by men became commonplace. It was awkward.

"Goodbye, Joey. You're the best friend I will ever have," he said.

Then he said something I'll always remember. Howie always told the truth. To a fault sometimes.

"Have a good life," he said.

"You, too," I said.

We split up and went our separate ways. As I entered the 9-14 classroom, I received a standing ovation. Apparently test scores had plummeted in my absence. The kids walked me to my desk. A package of Yankee Doodles was waiting for me. It was very sweet. Mrs. Scalise was happy to have me back as well. She asked me if I had finished my term paper and I said yes. She wanted me to read it to the class.

"Now?" I asked.

"If you're happy with it?" she answered.

If I was happy with it? What did that mean? I guessed it was writer speak.

"I'm happy with it," I said confidently.

I walked up to the front of the room and took out my paper. For some reason I wasn't nervous at all. I began reading out loud to the class. I looked up occasionally at their faces as I was reading, and they began to change. They seemed to go from anticipatory boredom to well, almost interested. Moved even. Especially when I got to the part my father was holding back.

"Then out of the trees come about twenty Vietcong, using spears, knives, anything they could get their hands on. My buddies began falling to the ground. We started firing back. Now the Vietcong are going down. It's bedlam. My gun jams, and a Vietcong sees his chance and comes at me, slashing away with his knife. I grab the knife away from him. It's a pocketknife. I plunge it into his stomach. And again. Like the knife your grandfather gave you. The one that couldn't hurt anybody. I bent down and turned him over. He was fifteen years old, Joey. Fifteen. It could've been you."

I stopped and looked up. There wasn't a dry eye in the house. Even Sal Glorioso was crying. I had done it. I had gotten the emotion.

I received an A+, and a big hug from Mrs. Scalise.

"You have a gift, Joseph. A real gift."

Right then I thought, I like this writing business. To have your words move people to tears. Forget construction, I'm going to be a writer. Case closed.

Telling Howie about moving was painful enough but how were we going to tell my grandfather. My father said he'd tell him, that I didn't need to be there. But that didn't seem right, it seemed cowardly. I was sixteen now, almost a man. And if you are a man, you must act like a man. I insisted I be part of the conversation to break the news to my grandfather. In hindsight maybe it wasn't the best decision I ever made. We chose to deliver the news at the New Deal restaurant. We figured it was a public place my grandfather would have to maintain some decorum. We went there, just the three of us. Three generations of Palumbo men.

The waiter met us at the door. He remembered us from last time.

"I know, three pork lo meins."

"Not this time," my father proudly said, "we'd like to see menus."

The waiter was surprised but pleased. He led us over to a booth by the front window. He handed us three menus.

"Can I get you gentlemen something to drink?" he asked.

"I'll have a double martini," my father said.

"Me, too," my grandfather said. The waiter looked at me.

"Lemonade," I said. "Make that a double."

I got a strange look from the waiter.

"Are we celebrating something? You get something from the architect?" my grandfather asked.

"No, Pop, I didn't." my father tugged at his collar, as if to say, is it hot in here or is it just me? Tell him, Dad, tell him.

"You'll like the food, Pop. We ate here last week. Didn't we, Joe?"

"Yeah, the pork lo mein is very good," I said.

Come on Dad tell him already.

"Pop, I like Brooklyn, don't get me wrong. Everybody together, Sunday dinners, it's been wonderful. But there comes a time when a man needs a change. To spread his wings, otherwise, he'll shrivel up and die," my father said.

"Danny, quit tap dancing, what's this about?" my grandfather asked.

Finally, I couldn't take it. I stood up.

208

"We're moving to Staten Island!" I blurted out.

Then I sat down, totally exhausted. All color drained from my grandfather's face. He had the same look Sidney Fishman had when I punched him in the stomach. A whiter shade of pale.

"I'm sorry, Pop," my father said. Then he tried to soften the blow. "I don't want you to worry about paying me anything for my share of the business. And whenever you decide, if you decide, to sell the property, you can give me whatever you want. Whenever you want."

My grandfather just sat there reading his menu. Not one word.

"I know this is hard. I wish things were better at work, but I've tried to get things going but it's just not happening," my father went on.

Still nothing. I tried to lighten the mood.

"Maybe you and grandma can move out there with us. We'll have lots of room and a pool. And grass. Green, green grass like at Ebbetts Field. What do you say?" I chipped in.

Still nothing.

"Pop don't do this, you should talk. Say something."

My grandfather put his menu down. Then he went on to speak with a clarity that I had never heard from him before. It was without rancor or anger, just direct like he was Perry Mason giving his closing argument.

"I don't understand this thing you have with Staten Island. You have a good business right here. All these old buildings will someday need remodeling, we just have to hang on. Everything you need is here. Your life is here," he said.

"We'll create a new life there. Like Grandpa Nunzio did when he moved from Palermo to Brooklyn," my father said.

"But what kind of life? You're taking Joey away from everything he knows. His school, his friends, his grandmother. *Me*," my grandfather said.

My father was about to cry. Me, too.

"Come with us, Pop. Sell everything and come," my father pleaded.

"No!" my grandfather said emphatically.

"Why not?" my father asked.

"Because my life is here," my grandfather said.

The waiter returned with the drinks. He put them down on the table. Then he stood there sensing the tension.

"You need more time?" he asked.

"No, we'll have three pork lo meins," I said.

We handed back the menus to the waiter who gave an 'I knew it' expression and he went off.

That had to be the coldest feeling meal I had ever sat through. I don't know what we talked about. Or if we talked. But the cat was out of the bag.

A few months passed. My mother found us a great house. Just what she wanted. It had everything, four bedrooms, a pool, and grass up the ying yang. Escrow was going to close the next week. And we'd be moving out of our apartment.

The night before we moved, I was lying in my bed looking at the ceiling one last time. I was feeling sad. And lonely. I couldn't leave Brooklyn without saying goodbye to Becky. I checked the clock; it was ten minutes to midnight. Too late to call. I sneaked out of my apartment and headed up 73rd street to The Le Parc. I climbed over the railing and went to her bedroom window. I tapped on it. Nothing. I peeked in, it was dark, Becky must be asleep. Maybe I shouldn't disturb her. Then I remembered what Coach Zeitchick used to tell me: "Be aggressive, Joey. You're a sweet kid but you're not going to get anywhere unless you are more aggressive." I wasn't sure if he was only referring to basketball or life in general, and it was too late to call him to check. I assumed he meant life and I went ahead and applied it to the situation I was in. I went to the window and 'aggressively' tried to open it. It wasn't budging, someone had painted it shut.

What to do, what to do? Ah hah. The Swiss Army knife, of course. What every good builder and sixteen-year old burglar should have. I loved the Swiss. Almost as much as the French. I took the knife out of my pocket and pulled out the cutting blade. I took the blade and ran it all around the edge of the bottom sash where it met the frame. It was working. Then I slowly lifted the window, and started to climb in. A light went on and Becky was standing over me with a baseball bat in her hands.

"Joey?" she asked.

"Yup, it's me," I said.

"What are you crazy? I could've killed you," she said.

What happened to the Jewish pacifist, I thought?

"I'm sorry, I just had to see you," I said.

She helped me inside. Then she closed the door. Turned on a lamp light. You guessed it, she had the same pajamas on, but this time I was ready for it. I looked at her face the whole time.

"Come sit," she said and patted the bottom of the bed. I sat down. She sat down by the pillow crossing her legs under her. God, I wished I could do that.

"I'm moving tomorrow," I said.

"I know, I heard from Howie," Becky confirmed.

We started to apologize to each other at the same time. Always a good sign.

"You first," she said.

"No, ladies first."

"I've been stubborn, Joey and I want to apologize for that. I know Sidney Fishman is a jerk. I'm sorry. I'm so sorry."

"Ah, it's okay. No harm, no foul, as they say."

"I wish that were true, but my actions prevented us from being together."

"Well we're together now," I said. Mr. Cool.

"Yes, we are," she said.

"What do you think we should do?" I asked.

Becky thought for a bit.

"I know, let's lie down on my bed and not make a sound and just hug each other," she said.

"Sure, I can do that," I said. "Not a problem."

So that's what we did. Hugged each other until it was time for me to go home. I left the same way I went in, through her window. And I went home.

Moving day, I had mixed emotions. I was sorry to leave but also excited in a way for what would come next. My father paid Ernie and some of the company's workers to help load the moving truck. Might as well keep it in the family so to speak. It didn't take long at all. That's the beauty of having an 800 square foot apartment. You can be out of there in a few hours. We left most of the old stuff, refrigerator, dining room set. Well that was practically new, nobody used it. But the rest was old, and my mother wanted to start new. We got rid of the Castro Convertible Sofa. Thank God. That was one thing I wouldn't miss.

The immediate family was there to see us off. My grandfather wouldn't or couldn't come out of the house. I saw my father head inside to say goodbye to him. He was holding the key to the apartment in his hand. I thought I'd tail along just in case he needed me. Although I didn't think I could be much help. Saying goodbye to my grandfather was too difficult for me. No words could express how much he meant to me, and how much I loved him. I went inside and pretended I had to go to the bathroom. I was in earshot of what was said by these two proud men. My grandfather was sitting at the head of the dining room table, alone, nursing a glass of wine. My father walked over to him.

"Well, Pop, we're taking off," he said as he placed the keys to the apartment on the table.

"I'm sure you won't have any problem renting the apartment. Especially with a new bathroom."

My grandfather just sat there sipping his wine.

"I'll call when I get there, let you know everything is alright. Bye, Pop." My father exited the house.

My grandfather was as close to crying as I ever saw him. I wanted to go to him and tell him everything was going to be okay, that we'd still come in for Sunday dinner and holidays, but I just stood there. Frozen. Then I heard a car horn. Honk, honk. I was being called. I headed for the door and left my grandfather there. Sitting alone with his back turned to me.

I came outside. My father was behind the wheel sobbing like a baby. I felt like crying myself but for some reason, I didn't. Maybe it was because everyone around me was crying so I couldn't. Someone had to be the designated non crier. I got in the back seat and held down my stereo next to me. My father started up the car. It died. He tried again. Nothing. Apparently, the car didn't want to go. Then he tried one more time and it started up. He gunned it; a cloud of smoke came out of the exhaust pipes. Final goodbyes. We were off. Hi-yo Silver, away!

"Watch out for the snakes. I hear they have big ones," Aunt Theresa called out.

I glanced back at the window of the bottom floor of the three-family brick house and looking out behind the curtain was my grandfather. He had a pained expression on his face. Then he turned away and disappeared.

Chapter 8

Trouble in Paradise

Staten Island Ferry

A good part of living in the new house was it was close to the Staten Island Ferry. The Ferry was not only free, it went directly to Manhattan. That's where I went a lot. By myself. Secretly. I had never done anything by myself. It was a totally new experience. In Brooklyn you never did anything alone. Always in pairs, sometimes in groups. The thought that you could go someplace far away by yourself was unfathomable. There I was, alone. No Howie, no Becky, no nobody. I did a lot of soul searching. Would I be a successful writer? What would I write? Books? Television? Movies? What if I wasn't good enough? The Ferry gave me the perfect place to contemplate these major life decisions. I got views of the Statue of Liberty, Lower Manhattan, Ellis Island. Every time I passed Ellis Island, I thought of Papa Nunzio. He came to a foreign land not knowing the language, no money, no job, one suit. What guts he had. How could I complain about going to Staten Island compared to what my great grandfather went through?

I loved the ferry. Service was twenty-four hours a day three hundred sixty-five days a year. It's a 5.2-mile run. Took about 25 minutes each way. I timed it. Yup, 25 minutes to the second. I didn't know a thing about Staten Island before we moved there that summer. My mother timed the close of escrow to be on July 1, her anniversary. I still didn't know what escrow meant but I knew we were able to move into our house after that date. Staten Island is one of the five boroughs that make up New York City. The residents call it the forgotten borough. Because like Rodney Dangerfield, "It can't get no respect." In Brooklyn we referred to it as the "sticks" and the "boonies." It was a good size, fifty-eight square miles to be exact, but it had no people. Well it had people, but they were spread out. Staten Island had the highest percentage of residents of Italian ancestry in the nation. The signs on coffee shops read, Caffe and on delicatessens, Salumeria.

Thank God I could still get my Yankee Doodles, otherwise I'm on the Verrazano bridge headed back to Brooklyn. After the Italians there were the crickets. Had millions of those. Then came the Irish, 14%, a few Germans, 6% and almost no Jews. I didn't know who I was going to hang out with. Where would I get my potato knishes? My blintzes? My Nathans' hot dogs? This was serious. I felt like I landed on the moon.

Luckily there was a lot of work to do moving in so I couldn't dwell on how much I missed my old life. We moved into a 4 bedroom 2 1/2 bath house with potential. That's real estate speak for a house ready to fall down. My father was feeling better. He even started going to a shrink. He began to control his anger. Plus, one of the main causes of his anger was gone. My grandfather. Another good part of living in Staten Island was I finally had my own bedroom. Uncle Joe delivered a Garofalo box spring and mattress as a housewarming gift to me. My dad and I set it up. We also hung a few pictures of my favorite ballplayers. Clyde Frasier and Dick Barnett. I was all set. Bedroom wise. My father left me alone in my new digs. I immediately started jumping up and down on the mattress like you do when you're six years old. Becky said I was making up for a lost part of my childhood. She was right, of course. Then I turned on my new color TV. I could watch Debbie Drake now and not worry someone was going to walk in on me. I could push a button and lock the door. But the funny thing was I was losing interest in her. I began to see her like other people did. Just a pretty lady who did exercises. What was happening to me? Is this typical of a sixteen-year-old? Is this what Staten Island did to you? Bored, I turned off the Debbie Drake show.

Then one day out of the blue it happened. I got a letter from Becky. A Dear Joe letter. She decided she wanted to be free to see 'other boys.' She said my living so far away changed everything. Blah, blah, blah. I was devastated. The phrase 'other boys,' kept repeating in my brain. I was out of the picture now. 'Other boys' didn't include me, the word 'other' operative. I got depressed. I began to really miss my old life again. I'd go to the ferry and stand up by the bow, the front, for you landlubbers. Let the ocean spray hit my face as the boat cut through the waves. I was in a word a mess. A pathetic mess.

I decided to act. I was going to head out to Smithtown to see my cousin Rosemary. She could shed light on the whole thing. She'd know what I'd been going through. She had to face the same set of problems. Coming from Brooklyn, being expected to follow the program set out for you.

My mother drove me to the Long Island Railroad. She was happy that I was moving forward, not moping around the house yearning for my old life. She was proud of me for going all the way to Smithtown alone. I knew I was in for a long trip, so I brought a stack of sports magazines, catch up with my reading. It was the first time I had been on the LIRR. They had a ticket taker who punched your destination. A conductor who announced each stop over a loudspeaker. Fancy schmancy. "Far Rockaway". I started reading my Sport Magazine. "Valley Stream." I'm on to baseball now. "Hempstead." Basketball. "Floral Park." I'm sleeping now. "Hicksville." I'm still sleeping. "Syosset." I'm looking out the window at the wide-open fields as we whiz by. "Cold Spring Harbor." I'm getting antsy now. "Huntington." Real antsy. "Greenlawn." I like lawns. Maybe I should get off here and walk the rest of the way. "Northpoint." Am I there yet? "Kings Park."

Please let this ride end. And finally, finally "Smithtown." I had made it.

Rosemary was there to pick me up. To say she was happy to see me would be a gross understatement. She kept kissing me. On the cheek, my forehead, my head. You can take a girl out of Brooklyn, but you can't take Brooklyn out of the girl. I was her favorite cousin she kept saying. We eventually got into her Volvo Station wagon. Now this was a solid looking vehicle. A foreign job. Not bad, I thought to myself. On the way to her house she talked and talked, telling me about her life in Smithtown. I remembered Uncle Joe calling her a boccalone, a 'Talking machine.' He used to pay her a quarter when she was young to stop talking. Smithtown hadn't changed her. But the amazing thing was she was interesting. Politics, art, music, boy girl relationships, careers, she knew something about everything.

"Are you sure you're not Jewish?" I kidded her.

"You know, Joe, as wonderful as living close to family is sometimes it can hold you back from discovering who you are. What you can accomplish. They see you a certain way, and you get comfortable with their vision of you. But it might not match your

222

vision of you. You have to strike out on your own to become the best Joey Palumbo you can be," she said.

Then she said something that has always stuck with me:

"There are a lot of ways to live a life, Joey. A lot of ways."

We arrived at her house. A four thousand square foot, five-bedroom brown shingled house with a library, a weight room, and a barn. My God, she had a horse. And chickens. A dog. Boo. One thing for sure, this wasn't Brooklyn. Or Staten Island even. Her husband, Bill was there to greet us. Bill was a principal at a high school. He was educated, cultured, intelligent, different from the men I was used to being around. Bill had Sunday dinner with the family once and he passed the test of my uncles eating out of his plate. From what I could tell, the family amused him, kinda like Jane Goodall and her apes. I could see Bill doing a dissertation on "The Palumbo Clan. A Case Study."

Bill had made us lunch, a Quiche Lorraine. I liked it.

"It's a French dish," Bill informed me.

As usual the French got it right. I told Bill one day I was going to go to France.

"Travelling is good, it broadens your horizons," Rosemary said, and you could tell she had heard that a thousand times from Aunt Nettie.

"You know, Joey, nobody in the family visits us. It's too far out they say. If we want to see the family, we have to go into Brooklyn, which we have done for a few Sunday dinners at Aunt Josie's. But nobody reciprocates. So, we wait for family weddings and funerals," she said.

Seemed sad to me. I was glad I was not so far away. After lunch we jumped in their car and I got the tour of Smithtown. Lots of lakes and reservoirs. But they're all called ponds for some reason. Willow Pond, Webster Pond, Millers Pond. Then we hit the parks, Maple Avenue Park my favorite, rolling hills, basketball courts with nets. We're talking nets like in the NBA nets.

Then we hit Bill's high school. Smithtown West. If there is a west that means, there's an east. It was like a college campus. Separate brick buildings, trees, flowers, a manicured baseball field with a running track. People live like this?

"You know Bob Costas, the baseball announcer is from Smithtown," Bill told me.

It was as if he was trying to get me to move there so Rosemary wouldn't miss the family so much. But we all knew that was an impossibility. After the tour we went back home and fed Boo and Rusty, the horse. I used a bow-line knot that I learned from the scouts to tie Rusty to a post so we could eat ourselves. Rosemary was impressed.

"You're good with animals," she said, "for a Brooklyn kid."

I smiled and thought to myself, I could get used to this life.

We packed a dinner and went to an outdoor movie theatre. A 'Drive in' they called it. We watched the movie from our car under the stars. We saw 'The Bridge on the River Kwai,' with Alec Guinness. A great flick.

"Be happy in your work," a line uttered by the Japanese commander of the prison camp rattled around in my brain for months. It was my first time watching a movie in a car. Kinda strange but fun also. Lots of action in the back seats of the cars. It made me miss the Marboro Theater and Becky. We stopped at Baskins and Robbins, had ice cream cones and then headed home. On the way home Rosemary fell asleep, from all the excitement of the day. Bill talked to me about my future.

"You'll have to switch over from vocational studies to an academic curriculum when you go to high school. I know some deans at colleges you might want to go to. Some with outstanding basketball programs. I might even be able to get you a scholarship. Colleges can always use a good point guard," he said with a smile.

For the first time I felt what it must have been like to be Jewish. To have someone taking this kind of interest in your education. It was tough to digest it all. But I certainly appreciated it.

I slept in their guest room. It wasn't on a Garofalo mattress so I couldn't sleep. Lots of thoughts floated around in my mind. Could I really go to college? Bill and Rosemary seemed to think so. So did Mr. Hunt, and Mrs. Scalise. Well then maybe I could.

The next day Bill and Rosemary drove me to the train station. They were sad to see me go. I promised to come back when the time was good. Bill had a book he wanted me to read, "Of Mice and Men," by John Steinbeck. I thanked him thinking it was a book about mice and men.

On the train ride home, I began reading that book. It was captivating, the characters brilliantly drawn. The whole thing was a new experience for me. I read the entire book by the time I reached home. Looking back, that visit to Smithtown was a seminal event in my life. I didn't know it at the time, but I will always be grateful to my cousins for opening the world to me.

My mother picked me up at the train station. On the way home I talked nonstop about my visit. What Bill had said about transferring to the academic block in high school and then going on to college. She was all for it.

"You got the head, as Aunt Theresa would say," she joked.

I could tell she felt guilty for not guiding me more in this area. But she did the best she could, like all the Italian parents in Brooklyn. The cards were stacked against them and the sorriest part was they didn't know it. We were raised with a kind of benign neglect. I wasn't about to complain. 'It takes a village to raise a child.' Thank God Rosemary and Bill were in my village. Anyway, I changed the subject and talked real estate. Always a safe topic. I couldn't help comparing my new house to Rosemary and Bill's. The Eddie Cantor song apropos:

"How ya gonna keep 'em down on the farm, after they've seen Pareee?"

But I was also a realist. That can come later in life. A goal to attain. For now, I had to be satisfied with what I had. My mother got our house for a steal from a guy who was being transferred to California. The best part was the front and the backyard. The front had a huge lawn. The back a huge pool. I had gotten my wish. This comes under the heading of 'Be careful what you wish for.' My father put me in charge of mowing and cleaning the pool. A veteran move by him.

"Is this great or what?" my mother would say as we all sat in the backyard looking out at the tranquil setting. And everyone agreed with her.

"The best, Mom, the best," I'd say.

As happy as my mother was, my father wasn't so thrilled. He was glad to be away from my grandfather's dominance, but he also felt like a Benedict Arnold. Leaving his father alone with a failing business weighed heavily on him. Loyalty was everything in Brooklyn. Fairness and loyalty jockeying for dominance. Uncle Sal hired my father to be his foreman on a big shopping center he was building. So, my father kept busy. But when he was home, I'd catch him staring off in the distance with a sadness in his eyes. He missed the old way of life, too.

We started off going home for Sunday dinner, but then we went less and less. My mother had to hold open houses on Sunday, the traffic across the bridge was too much, the pool needed cleaning, you know the story. But we did keep up the tradition of Sunday dinner, only now it was in Staten Island. Not the umpteen courses that my grandmother provided, but a scaled down version. Uncle Sal and Bernice and new baby, Salvatore came. My grandparents never came, it was considered enemy territory, and Aunt Theresa was afraid of bridges.

"What if it collapses right when I'm going over it?" she fretted.

My father and I would barbecue. Hamburgers, steaks, baked potatoes. I liked to cook. Gave me a chance to think.

"Dad, I'd like to be a writer like John Steinbeck. Write novels."

"Joe, you can be anything you want. But you have plenty of time to figure it out. You're putting too much pressure on yourself. For now, just enjoy being a boy."

Great advice. I felt a giant weight had been lifted from my shoulders. I was feeling pretty good that Sunday. Until the roof caved in. Not literally, figuratively.

We were sitting at a long glass top table, on black wrought iron chairs. A huge umbrella kept the sun's rays at bay. Citronella did the same with the mosquitoes. That was also on the list, a screened in porch.

"Is this the life or what?" Uncle Sal said.

Uncle Sal couldn't have been happier having family on this side of the bridge.

"When you pare it all away, get down to it, family is the only thing that matters. Friends are great but they come and go. Family is forever," Uncle Sal said.

"And we have you to thank for us being here. We never could've come up with all that cash," my mother said.

"Don't thank me. Danny's the one who should be thanked. He made the decision to move," Uncle Sal reminded us.

These words made my father uncomfortable. He would always change the subject.

"Another hot dog, Uncle Sal?" he asked deflecting the conversation. Uncle Sal looked at Bernice. She shook her head no.

"Sure, why not? My cholesterol count's already through the roof, what's one more hot dog," Uncle Sal said, half joking.

My father headed over to the grill. All eyes on him.

"Sunday's are the hardest. It took me years before I could get through a Sunday without crying," Uncle Sal whispered.

"I have the hankies to prove it," Bernice added while breast feeding baby Sal.

"With Danny it's the whole week. He goes through the motions, does his job, but he feels like a captain who abandoned a sinking ship," my mother said.

"I've offered to lend Vince money, Gina. What else can I do?" asked Uncle Sal.

"I don't know," my mother agreed.

"He's the most stubborn man I've ever known. He won't ask for help," Uncle Sal lamented.

"Maybe you shouldn't wait to be asked?" Bernice said.

Everyone looked at her. You know, the quiet one, may be on to something.

Just then the phone rang. My father already up, answered it. He mostly listened. Suddenly his face turned ashen, like when you are hit with unexpected bad news. He hung up the phone and returned to the table, handed Uncle Sal his hot dog.

"What's wrong, Dan?" my mother asked.

"Nothing," he said. "We'll talk about it later."

"Dan..."

"My father has prostate cancer," my father said.

"Oh jeez," Uncle Sal said, almost choking on his hot dog.

"Oh, Danny, I'm so sorry," my mother said. "Go. You have to go."

"I'll take care of everything here," Uncle Sal offered.

"You sure?" my father asked.

"I'm sure," he said.

"I'd like to go, too," I chimed in.

"Sure, take Joey with you," my mother said to my father.

Uncle Sal put his arms around my father and me.

"Take as long as you need," he said.

The next morning, we headed back to Brooklyn. I had my permit to drive now and all I needed was a licensed driver in the car. My father had been going places with me in Staten Island and I was getting pretty good. But we were on a serious mission, my father was in no mood to play driving instructor.

"Is Grandpa going to die?" I asked worried what could be the worst thing that could happen.

"Joey, your grandfather's not going to die. If anyone can beat this he can," my father assured me.

"He can't die. I won't let him," I said as if I had the power over life and death.

We pulled up in front of the house. The white magnolia tree still on guard along with the pink flamingoes. We exited the car, suitcases in tow. My grandmother was waiting for us outside, on the bench. She was so relieved to see us. She kept kissing us, going from one cheek to the other. I was used to it by now from cousin Rosemary. She led us inside to Aunt Jenny's room. It was all set up. Two single beds. Aunt Jenny was staying at Rudy's. My grandmother wasn't thrilled with that notion, after all they weren't married yet, but they were engaged, and this was no time to quibble about appearances.

My grandfather was outside in his shop sanding something. Looked like tiny figurines. We had some time, so we unpacked and had a couple of meatball sandwiches on Italian bread and two Dr. Brown's orange sodas. Boy I missed my grandmother's cooking.

"How's he doing, Ma?" my father asked.

"He won't talk about it. He pretends he's fine. He sees Dr. Chen, tomorrow at 10AM," she said.

"A Chinese surgeon? That must have gone over big," my father said.

"He almost cancelled six times," she said.

I looked out the window watching my grandfather work. It was hard to imagine him sick. He never got sick. He was Hercules and Superman, rolled into one.

My grandfather finally came inside. He wasn't crazy about us being there, a sign of weakness in the strong man world. But he also knew that my father was the kind of guy you wanted in your corner when the chips were down.

"Thanks for coming, Danny," he said quietly.

The next morning, I drove my father's truck to the hospital. My grandfather and father squeezed in next to me in the front seat. The ride was smooth, my grandfather was impressed, but still a little apprehensive after the last time we drove together. I passed Seth Low Park on the way. It was deserted, except for the old men playing chess. I noticed a few Chinese kids playing basketball on the 'A' court. Things had changed or were at least changing.

I made a left on Avenue O and passed The Le Parc. The first thing I noticed was the outside brick work got a much-needed face lift. Apparently recent immigrants from India had a new business going. They would power wash the bricks on the face of the building and retool the grout bringing it back to its original condition. Find a need and fill it, isn't that the American way. I found out later that most of these workers had top positions in India, army officers, teachers, government workers, but when they came here this is what they had to do. I admired their enterprising spirit. Work is sacred and nothing was beneath them.

Then my father spoke. Out of the silence.

"I'll handle things from now on," he said.

My grandfather nodded.

"The business. Everything. You understand?" he said.

Again, my grandfather nodded.

I was witnessing a changing of the guard. My father, the prince, was becoming King even though the King was still alive.

My father had told me earlier of a dream he had that first night in Aunt Jenny's bedroom.

"We were all seated around the dining room table. Everybody. Grandpa, Grandma, Aunt Theresa, Aunt Jenny, Rudy, Uncle Tommy, Uncle Sal, Bernice, your mom, you, and me. Even Papa Nunzio was there on a chair off to the side. As if to witness something important about to happen. Your grandpa is seated at the head of the table as usual. Suddenly, he gets up. He asks me to change seats with him. It's as if he knew he was dying, and he wanted me to take over as the head of the family." I didn't usually believe in hocus pocus stuff but there's no denying the relevance of that dream.

We arrived at Coney Island Hospital at 2601 Ocean Parkway. Hospitals in Brooklyn must be experienced to be believed. More chaos than order, people coming and going, patients, doctors, nurses, visitors, staff all intertwining until you couldn't tell who was who. I parked the truck and we entered through a revolving door. My father had to go to the bathroom. Hey, Mr. Head of the family, where you going? My grandfather and I stepped up to the receptionist. A black girl, dripping with personality, Wanda Matthews, the name on her badge.

"Who are you here to see?" she asked.

My grandfather looked at me.

"Dr. Chen," I said, "the surgeon."

"Is he your mouthpiece?" the receptionist joked.

"He's my grandson," my grandfather deadpanned.

"Insurance?" she asked.

"Yes," he said.

He just stood there.

"May.. I... see... your... card?" she asked

My grandfather took out his wallet. Yup there she was, in clear plastic. He handed it over to her.

"Don't use it much, do you?" she asked rhetorically.

"No, he doesn't," I piped up, "he's very healthy. Otherwise."

She smiled, handed back his card.

"Have a seat, we'll call you," she said.

We sat. We waited. My father soon joined us, and we waited some more. Finally, a nurse came out.

"Palumbo."

Like the Three Stooges the three of us got up. My grandfather walked over alone to her and she escorted him in with the usual pleasantries.

"How are you this morning?" she asked cheerily.

What a crazy greeting I thought. If he was any good, he wouldn't be here. My father and I sat back down and waited some more. And waited and waited and waited. I had exhausted all their sports magazines. Sports Illustrated, Sports Weekly, Sports Monthly, Baseball Digest, Basketball Digest, Pro Football Weekly, Pro Football Monthly, Lacrosse. Lacrosse? How'd that get in there? I looked for a novel since I had torn down that wall, but not a one. Then I picked up a New York Post newspaper. I looked at the ads. I couldn't help thinking of this kid from the neighborhood, Jerry Lowe. He got a job in Manhattan at an employment agency. He put an ad in the New York Post classifieds wanting to attract applicants for a position he purposely didn't mention.

"All that is needed is an interest in sports," it read.

He got over two million responses.

I later found out the job he had in mind was selling World Book Encyclopedias. Of course, the ad was misleading, actually a lie, but I'll never forget the genius of those words. Know your audience.

It was now 1:30PM. The waiting room had thinned out. We had been there over four hours. Not a good sign. Finally, Dr. Chen came out in his scrubs. We jumped up from our chairs to meet him. He pulled down his mask. He was sweating, he looked spent.

"We had to remove his prostate. But there are still some cancer cells in the prostate bed, the area where the old prostate used to be," he said clearly in perfect English.

"What's the next step?" my father wanted to know.

"We can use a combination of radiation and chemotherapy," the Doc said.

"Will that work?" my father asked.

"I don't know. There's some spots on a few lymph nodes, we're hoping the cancer doesn't spread," he said.

"When can we take him home?" I asked.

"In a few days," he responded.

"Thanks, Doc," my father said.

"Yeah, thanks," I said, my feeble attempt at being grown-up.

"I hope he didn't say anything out of line," my father wondered.

"Not at all. In fact, he paid me a compliment," the Doc said cheerfully.

"Oh?" my father said.

"He said my people did a pretty good job building that wall in China. I didn't want to ruin it by telling him I was born in Hoboken," he joked.

We all laughed. I liked this guy. And he wasn't Jewish. I might have to rethink my views on doctors.

"Oh, one more thing," the Doc said. "He's lost some weight. He's very concerned. I wouldn't bring it up."

Then he looked directly at me: "Capisce?" he said.

I nodded. I really liked this guy. I drove the two of us home. On the radio the Beatles, sang "Help" which matched the predicament we felt ourselves in. When we got home, we filled my grandmother in. Told her mum's the word on any weight loss. She was sad, of course, but all things considered she handled the news well. Stoic, almost. It was like she reached down deep inside herself and decided she was going to maintain a positive, hopeful attitude.

She wanted to go visit him right away. I offered to take her, but she refused.

"You've done enough," she said to me.

Uncle Tommy wound up taking her. They only could stay an hour, hospital rules, then they came back home.

That night we held a family meeting. My father was clearly in charge. In fact, he sat in my grandfather's chair. My mother came into Brooklyn to lend her support.

"What's next, Dan?" she wanted to know.

"Let's just go about things as usual. One thing my father hates is to be pitied. If there are any problems come to me."

"Whatever you say, Dan," Aunt Jenny agreed.

"If there is anything I can do, let me know," Rudy offered.

"Thanks, Rudy," my father said appreciatively. "I'm going back to Staten Island with Gina for a few days, take care of some business at the shopping center, but you can reach me by phone," my father instructed us.

"The weight, Dad. Tell 'em about the weight," I said.

"Oh, right. The doctor said he's concerned about his weight. Pop's regularly around 190. Let's tell him that's what he weighs if he asks. No use making him worry unnecessarily. Any questions?" he asked.

"I have a question," Aunt Theresa said.

"Sure, Aunt Theresa," my father said. "What is it?"

"Can I still watch my soap operas?" she asked.

Everybody cracked up.

"Sure, Aunt Theresa you can still watch your soap operas," my father assured her.

The next day I saw my father and mother off at the curb.

"Here's some money," he said.

My father gave me about a hundred dollars, just in case.

"You're my eyes and ears now, Joe. Keep me posted on anything that comes up," he instructed me.

My father handed me the keys to the truck and he and my mother took off in her brand-new Imperial Crown Convertible Chrysler. Apparently, another few escrows had closed.

As I stood there on the street waiting for them to disappear up 21st avenue a voice came in my head.

"Hey, what are you leaving me here for?"

That line came from an Untouchables episode. Some mobsters dropped off a stool pigeon at an abandoned warehouse at the dock. After they drove off leaving him alone there he called after them: "Hey, what are you leaving me here for?" A few seconds later a black sedan showed up, a machine gun poked out the window and he was riddled with bullets.

That's how I felt. I looked around for the black sedan to show but none did. I felt somewhat relieved and went inside.

For the next few days I hung out in the streets. I played in a football game. Two hand touch. They let me quarterback. I made a play. Drew it out with my finger on my sweatshirt.

"Davey take two steps over the middle and then turn I'll hit you. And you, Jimmy? You go long," I said.

Then it hit me. I was telling this kid to 'go long' to get him out of the way. I had no intention of ever passing him the ball. All the memories came rushing back of the times in my childhood that I told a kid to 'go long.' How mean was that? I felt bad about myself and vowed to make amends. Too late to go back in time but I could get this kid in the next play.

"Okay, Jimmy, this time you go five steps and buttonhook and I'll hit you. Make sure you're in the end zone."

I took the snap, lofted the ball, TOUCHDOWN! You should have seen this kid. He was literally dancing in the street he was so happy. I want to take this opportunity to apologize to all the kids in Brooklyn that I told to "go long," I am so sorry. Please forgive me.

After football, I passed a stickball game in progress. I couldn't resist.

"Hey, Nicky, can I have a swing?" I asked, calling on my athletic reputation to get me one swing of the bat.

"Sure, Joey. Hey, Ira, move back... Back... Back. To the blue Chrysler, ya moron."

Nicky pitched me a pink ball called a 'Spaldeen' on one bounce. WHACK. I hit the ball square. It sailed up and up and bam, smashed right through Mr. Resnick's window. Uh oh. I would've gladly paid for the broken window but there was no dealing with Mr. Resnick. It was like he was hoping it would happen. One, two, three, I knew it was coming... four, five. The window flew open and Mr. Resnick, wearing his usual holey t-shirt and protruding curly chest hair, stuck his head out.

"You sons of bitches. How many times have I told you not to play stickball in the street?" he yelled down.

Then he ducked his head back in and in a flash came back with a heavy pot filled with hot water. He heaved the hot water out the window and us boys scattered in all directions.

I decided it was safer at Seth Low Park. It was hot, hotter than I remembered. I was just shooting around, when David Sutton showed up. A Syrian kid who was a big fan of mine.

"Hey, Joey?" he said. "Wanna play one on one?"

Everyone needed a David Sutton in their life. Someone who worships the ground you walk on, thinks you're the greatest thing since chopped liver. He saw all my games at the JCH when I played for the Nobles, watched me in the park, all the Seth Low Jr. High School basketball games. He 'oohed and aahed' at the no look passes underneath. Called out "count it" when the ball left my hand for a bank shot. I vividly remembered the Seth Low Jr. High championship game. We were playing an away game against Francis Scott Key from Fort Green, Brooklyn. A tough team, an even tougher neighborhood. Very few kids from my school could make the away game. Or were afraid to make it.

But not David. He cut class and showed up before the team took the floor. He clapped wildly when we came out to do our layup drill. Scott Key was a talented team. All black players. Tall, athletic. Almost everyone could dunk. Their layup drill was designed to intimidate the opposition. It worked. Especially when their center dunked two balls at the same time at the end of the drill.

Seth Low had mostly Jewish kids, me and one black player. Harold Brown. Harold was a cut up. During practice he would sneak behind you and push the back of your knees with the front of his. And you'd sink in place. He thought that was the funniest thing in the world.

I also remember he lived in the projects and was sometimes afraid to go home after a late practice. I remember thinking what's he afraid of, he's black. Shows how little I knew. Most crime was black on black.

Anyway, Harold played his best game of the year. Sixteen points, eight rebounds. But it was our star player, Barry Erdos who won the game for us. The score was tied, Seth Low had the ball. Ten seconds left. The coach, Mr. Rhodes called time.

"Joey, get the ball to Barry. Got it?"

I wasn't paying as much attention as I should have.

"Joey are you listening to me?" he yelled two inches from my face. Hey, you can't do that, only Italians can do that. I was listening, but I was also looking around the gym. We will have a lot of unhappy people to deal with. I thought of the bus. What if it didn't start? Or even worse what if it was hijacked.

"Palumbo!" he yelled, trying to get my attention.

"I got it, coach," I said, "get the ball to Barry. Don't worry."

Coach was a big worrier. Must be hard to have your livelihood depend on a bunch of sixteen-year olds in shorts. Larry Slotnick was set to inbound the ball at half court. I ran to Slotnick and he practically handed me the ball. I dribbled it to the right wing and practically handed the ball to Barry. This was more like football than basketball. Then I cleared out of Barry's way. Barry faked a jump shot, got his defender in the air, and drove to the hoop. He swooped in for a finger roll. Game over. We won.

The gym went silent and David went nuts. He was running around the gym telling anyone who'd listen what a great pass I made. Pass? It was a handoff. From quarterback to half back. David gave me his personal MVP award for the game.

In short, he was my biggest fan. So that day I was worried about my grandfather and needed a pick me up, so I thought, why not?

"Sure," I said, "I haven't played in a while, so don't expect much."

"That's okay, I'll go easy on you," he kidded me.

We began to play. David was hitting everything he threw up. He must have been practicing a lot. He was never this good. Winners get the ball out in one on one, so he was piling up the score. I couldn't hit the broad sign of a barn. Air balls, missing my usually deadly backboard shots, clanging shots off the rim. The score was 10 to 1 in David's favor. Eleven won. David couldn't believe it. He was one point away from beating his hero. He was on cloud ten, cloud nine not high enough. Now I hated to lose, you gotta know that about me. A good boy sure but put a basketball in my hands and I became someone else. A competitive lunatic. One of the reasons my mother never came to a game, she didn't want to see that boy.

At this point it became a life and death struggle. David missed a jumper, a game clincher. I got the rebound. I raced to the top of the key. Swish, I sank a jump shot. It was now 10-2, my ball. I hit another jumper. Then banked one from the side, then a hook, calling out, "Houbregs." Then "Barnett, from the key." I drove past David for a layup. And another. Soon the score was 10-9.

David knew he was beat. His hero was hot, and he was showing no mercy. I did my patented move of dribbling in and then pulling back out. Nothing but net. It was 10-10. Sudden death. Whoever got the next point won. David was a sheep about to be slaughtered.

David handed me the ball. I dribbled around the key, back and forth, looked in David's eyes and thought what this loss would do to him... and I shot and missed. On purpose. David couldn't believe I finally missed a shot. He got the ball and dribbled around at the circle. I played enough defense so he wouldn't realize I was going to let him score. David shot and missed. I let him get the rebound and David laid it in. Game Sutton!

Well to say he was happy would have been the understatement of all time. He was as happy as Nelson Mandella must have been after being released from prison for 27 years. He danced around, hooted and hollered. Clapped hands. Patted me on the back.

"Can't win them all, Joe. Maybe next time."

I pretended to be disappointed I lost, congratulated him on his improved play and took my ball and went home. It was and still is the single best thing I have ever done in my life.

I still had some time to kill so I thought I'd visit Uncle Nicky and Aunt Dora. I hadn't said goodbye to them mainly because they were a difficult couple to be around. Constant arguing. I couldn't remember one thing they agreed on. Nowadays they would have gotten a divorce but in those days you stayed married. Period.

Aunt Dora also read tarot cards and although I really didn't believe in such things whenever I went over there, she read my cards.

"You're going on a trip; I see a lot of money in your future. Have you thought about snake charmer as a career?" Madame Dora would say.

Since choosing a career was always on my mind, despite the fact I had chosen to be a writer, I thought, sure why not? So, I walked on over there. They lived on 86th street and 20th avenue. I thought about driving but then I'd have to find a licensed driver to sit with me and that was too big a pain. So, I walked. It felt good to walk. In Staten Island you were in a car most of the time one of the main reasons my grandfather hated the place.

Uncle Nicky owned a pizza parlor. Pizza Palace. They lived upstairs from the store. Whenever I went over there the smell of cheese pizza permeated the house. Luckily, I liked the smell. I walked up the stairs and peeked in the open door.

"Joey?" my aunt asked.

"It's me," I said.

"Come, come in," she said.

I went inside. The house was cluttered with knick knacks, bric-a-brac. Alright junk.

"Place looks great," I said.

"I try," she said, proud of the decorating. "I heard about your grandfather. How's he feeling?"

"He's doing good. I pick him up tomorrow," I said.

"You want pizza? I got one fresh out of the oven," she said.

"Sure," I said. "Can't wait."

Uncle Nicky made unbelievably great pizza. It made up for having to go over there. Well almost. I sat down at her table and she presented me with my pizza. I was eating it, 'oohing and aahing' and she was staring at me. I didn't know what to say to her.

"How's Uncle Nicky?" I finally asked.

"He drives me crazy but what else is new. I think he was raised by wolves. Really," she complained.

"That's funny," I said. "I'll have to remember that."

"You want me to read your cards?" she asked.

"Sure," I said.

She whipped out a deck from her smock pocket. Started shuffling.

"What do you want to know?" she asked me.

"I want to know if writing should be my forever career or should I go with construction? I need confirmation. But if the cards say I should do something else just let me know," I said.

"Oh, that's an easy one," she said.

She turned over six cards.

"What do you see?" I asked.

She picked up some of the cards and began tossing them on the floor.

"You don't need that one and that one. You don't like to fly, so a pilot is out," she said.

"Is this allowed, Aunt Dora?" I asked.

"You want to choose the right career, right?" she responded sharply.

Just then Uncle Nicky showed up. He was in a tee shirt. He was sweating profusely from being near the ovens.

"Hi Uncle Nicky," I said

"Hey Joey, come stai?" he said, happy to see me. Or anybody really.

"Bene," I said, keeping in the Italian theme.

"Put on a shirt," Aunt Dora said to him.

"I'm making pizzas, I don't need a shirt," he replied.

"Put on a shirt. We have company," she said.

"Joey doesn't care if I wear a shirt, right, Joe?

"Well, I don't know, it's uh, up to, uh, you know," I said not wanting to get in the middle.

"What are you doing putting the kid on the spot? Now go put on a shirt," she said.

"I'm not putting on a shirt," he proclaimed.

"No shirt, no pizza," she said.

"I've had it with shirts," he said.

"I said put on a shirt," she demanded.

"I said no more shirts," he said.

Going over there was risky. I had to make my exit.

"I should leave, I'm picking up my grandfather tomorrow and I have to rest. But thanks for the pizza."

I skedaddled out of there. As I was running down the stairs, I heard them still arguing. I decided I was just going to have to confirm my career choice another way. An evening with Uncle Nicky and Aunt Dora was just not worth it.

Chapter 9

The Final Curtain

Ellis Island
The people Emma Lazarus had in mind.

I had some time before I picked up my grandfather from the hospital. I decided to go see the Statue of Liberty for inspiration. Uncle Tommy was working so I decided to take a chance and drive myself. 'Give me your tired, poor. Your huddled masses yearning to breathe free. The wretched refuse of your teeming shore. Send these, the homeless, tempest tossed to me. I will lift my lamp besides the golden door.' Emma Lazarus.

Now that was what I called good writing. Mrs. Scalise would have been proud of Emma; she got the emotion. I sat in my car looking up at the Statue that the French gave the United States. I wondered what inspired such a gift. Did they want something in return? Or was it pure generosity? As I contemplated these questions, I checked my watch. Yikes. I had to pick up my grandfather.

I sped to the hospital. The whole time I was looking in the rear-view mirror worried that a cop would stop me. It was a good lesson for me. Much easier to pay attention to the time and obey the law. My cousin, Lenny was right, I was a stiff. I arrived just in time. They brought my grandfather out in a wheelchair. This one-time Superman now reduced to a mere mortal. It was tough to see. The orderly helped him get up, but he motioned he didn't need his help.

"I can do it," my grandfather said.

He got in the truck by himself. I was figuring to take him home, but he had other plans.

"Take me to the bank. On Bay Parkway."

"The bank? Now? Shouldn't you be resting?" I said.

"I feel fine. Take me to the bank," he ordered me.

I drove to the bank, parked in front by a meter. My grandfather put a quarter in, and we went inside. We headed right over to a desk. Branch Manager, Carl

Felton. Carl stood up and warmly greeted my grandfather. My grandfather proudly introduced me.

"This is my grandson, Joey."

We shook hands. His hand was soft. Like a banker. I was sure he showered before work, not after. We all sat down.

"So, what can I do for you?" Carl asked.

"I'd like to cash in my Certificates of Deposits," my grandfather said.

The manager checked his files.

"Mr. Palumbo, they don't become due for another three months," he said.

"I know. But I need the money now," my grandfather said firmly.

"There'll be severe penalties for early withdrawal," Carl felt obliged to inform him.

"I know," my grandfather tried to assure him he knew what he was doing.

"You sure now?" Carl asked.

"This is my money, right?" my grandfather asked, getting a bit perturbed.

"Yes, of course," Carl said.

"Okay, then, I'd like to have it," he said.

My grandfather was done quibbling and Carl knew it.

"Whatever you say, Mr. Palumbo."

The manager accompanied my grandfather to the back and my grandfather opened his safe deposit box. He pulled out a few certificates. Then my grandfather went over to a teller and handed her the certificates. I assumed to deposit in his account. I heard that much. Then my grandfather went back to the bank manager and asked if he could make a local phone call.

"Sure, no problem," Carl said.

I couldn't hear the actual phone call as my grandfather spoke in a hushed voice. But I did hear the words Staten Island. I knew very well that I'd have to take him across the Verrazano Bridge if that's where he wanted to go. He hung up and came over to me.

"Come on, Joe, we're going to take a little ride," he said.

We drove awhile. After speeding back to the hospital, I drove in the right lane on the bridge. Slow. A man in his car pulled up next to me and yelled out his window: "Does that car have an accelerator?"

"Don't listen to him. You're doing fine," my grandfather said.

It seemed like it was taking forever. Finally, a sign, "Welcome to Staten Island."

"Where're we going, Grandpa?" I asked.

"I'll let you know when we get there," he said.

He pulled out of his pocket a tiny piece of paper where he'd written something. An address, I presumed. He began to look in the glove compartment, rummaging around, then he pulled out a map. He put on his specs and started to figure the route.

"Okay, make a right at the next exit," he said.

I put on my blinker right away. I knew you're supposed to be 100 feet from the exit, but I couldn't wait. I wanted to give people ample warning. My grandfather then proceeded to give me a bunch of commands. Left by the light, go straight, make a right here, no not yet, here. Finally, he told me to pull over to a door to a warehouse.

"We're here," he said.

"Here where?" I asked.

"Jimmy Giambo's warehouse. We're going to pay him the money we owe him," he said.

"But he took the backhoe back," I reminded him.

"Doesn't matter, you owe somebody, you pay him. You do the right thing," he said.

They walked in a door that said 'Office.' Boxes still unpacked. A metal desk, a few mismatched chairs. A fake ficus potted plant. Looks like Debbie Drake's decorator was there. Jim Giambo looked up from his paperwork and spotted us. He practically jumped out of his chair.

"Hey, Vince, what brings you to this neck of the woods?" he asked.

"I want to pay my bill for the backhoe," he said.

"What bill?" Jimmy asked.

"My bill, for the four months. I want to pay it," my grandfather said.

"You already paid it," Jimmy said.

"No, I didn't," my grandfather said.

"Your brother-in-law Sal paid it," Jimmy explained.

"What?" my grandfather exclaimed.

"I thought you knew," Jimmy said.

"I didn't know. Come on, Joey, we have work to do," my grandfather said.

We headed out. I had to run to keep up with him. I thought this guy had just been operated on. Isn't there supposed to be a recovery period? And what happened to my father taking over things? We headed back to Brooklyn. Across the Verrazano bridge again. This was more driving than I'd done in the three months I had my learner's permit. We went straight for the office. My grandfather went right over to Aunt Jenny.

"Show me a list of every supplier Sal paid," he demanded.

He was holding a hanky to his mouth. He was coughing.

"Pop take it easy," she said.

"Never mind take it easy. Show me the list," he insisted.

She opened a drawer and pulled out a sheet of paper.

"Read me the names. Please," my grandfather said.

"Grillo's Lumber, Mahoney Steel, Ghilotti Concrete, Jackson's..." she read.

"Son of a bitch," he fumed.

"...Hardware, and Garcia Disposal. That's it," Aunt Jenny finished.

"Here's what I want you to do. You repay Sal every penny. Every single penny. You understand?" he demanded.

"Sure, Pop, but what're we going to use for money?" Aunt Jenny wanted to know.

My grandfather started coughing more.

"We have money. I put money in the corporation account. Right, Joe?" he said.

"Right, we went to the bank and cashed in all of Grandpa's personal CD's," I said.

My grandfather shot me a look. "What are you the town crier?"

"You shouldn't have done that, those were for when you retire," Aunt Jenny scolded.

"I have cancer, Jenny," he reminded her. "Cancer!!"

I drove my grandfather home. He was coughing more now. All the activity catching up with him. My grandmother immediately brought him into their bedroom and started to help him put on his pajamas.

"We don't take charity. Not now, not ever," he said, as he coughed.

"He was just trying to help. Here, drink this," she said.

He gulped down that water like he had just come out of the Sahara Desert. He calmed down.

"Yeah, well I don't need his help," he said. "I have to go to the bathroom."

I found his slippers under the bed. put them on his feet.

"My brother meant well, Vince," my grandmother said.

"He should've asked. I've never borrowed from family. I'm not starting now," he hollered.

"Okay, you made your point. All this yelling isn't doing you any good," she said.

You want yelling you should go over to Uncle Nicky and Aunt Dora's house, I thought.

My grandfather wanted to see how much he weighed. We all squeezed into the bathroom. My grandfather got on the scale. My grandmother got on her knees looking at the dial.

"I can do that, Grandma," I said.

"No, it's easy for me I've been on my knees my whole life," she said.

But I knew the real reason she wanted to do it; she didn't want me to have to lie.

"What does it say?" he asked.

She looked at the dial. I could see it from where I was standing. It read 180.

"The same," she said.

"How much?" he demanded to know.

"One hundred ninety."

"You sure?" he asked.

"Of course, I'm sure. What, I can't read a scale?" she said. "Come on I want you in bed. Enough with the scale," she said.

He got in bed. He let me take off his slippers and I helped to pull the covers over him. I tucked him in. That was a first for me.

That night my grandparents ate their meal on the outside table in the backyard. I remember her helping him put on his napkin like you do with a baby. Such a tender moment and one I will remember all my life.

We continued to stay with my grandfather nursing him back to health and taking him to his radiation and chemotherapy appointments. My father would come and go but I stayed. I watched my grandfather like a hawk. I would see him looking in the mirror trying to determine whether he was looking thinner. But my grandmother continued the ruse they had set up.

Then one day I was called into action. We were sorting wine bottles in the basement. My grandfather was on the ladder and I was holding it as usual. He was looking a little shaky to me. He almost lost his footing.

"Hey, be careful, Grandpa. You fall, I get in trouble. I can do that," I offered.

"Nah. You hold the ladder," he said. He sorted a few more bottles, almost falling again.

"I can do it, Grandpa. Really."

"Okay, okay. You do it," he finally gave in.

He climbed down off the ladder and I took a few bottles off the table and climbed up. The new replaces the old, or at least the sick. My grandfather was now holding the ladder.

"Joey?" he called up the ladder.

"What?" I asked.

"I peed in my pants," he said sheepishly.

"Oh," I said.

I could see he was mortified. I knew he was wearing diapers. I also knew the last thing he wanted me to see was him in a diaper. Incontinence was a side effect of having your prostate removed.

"That's okay, Grandpa, you go change, I can do this myself," I said.

My grandfather went to the bathroom upstairs where he could change his diaper in private. I began to do the sorting myself. It was really a one-man job but clearly more fun with two. Like most work. Before I was done on the ladder my grandfather came downstairs carrying the scale. Uh oh.

"Come down, I want you to help me do something," he said.

"Okay, Grandpa," I said.

I climbed down the ladder. Oy gevald, I thought to myself. Sometimes I thought in Yiddish. My grandfather put the scale down on the floor and stepped up on it.

"I want you to tell me how much I weigh," he asked.

I would rather be walking on a hot bed of coals.

"Maybe I can go get Grandma, she's good at this," I said.

"No! You're the only one I trust. How much?" he asked.

The scale read 178. He was losing weight. I tried delay tactics. I started wiping the little glass cover with my shirt.

"Gotta clear this off. It's a little scratched," I said.

"What does it say?" he wanted to know.

I was torn. I was the only one he trusted so I didn't want to lie. But I didn't want to tell him the truth either.

"190, Grandpa. Exactly," I said with conviction.

"You sure now?" he asked.

"Yeah, Grandpa, I'm sure. I gotta go," I said.

I ran up the basement stairs and headed to the backyard. My grandmother was picking figs off the tree.

I went over to her. My eyes had watered, I was trying not to cry. I blamed Uncle Sal for my propensity to cry. He started it.

"What's wrong, Joey?" she asked.

"I lied to Grandpa about his weight," I said, still holding back the tears.

"You did the right thing," she assured me.

"Then how come I feel so bad?" I wondered.

"Come here," she said, and she held out her arms. I went to her.

"It's okay to cry," she said, "it doesn't make you any less of a man."

By then I was crying uncontrollably. It wasn't only the lying that hurt but it was the realization my grandfather was fading, and I could lose him.

"Help me pick these. We don't want to waste any figs," my grandmother said.

The next day my father came in and we went to the yard to check things out. A job that had been keeping them afloat had come to an end. Ernie was unloading the unused wood and stacking it in a rack. We went up to him. Big hellos.

"How's your father?" Ernie asked.

"Hanging in there," my father said.

"Good, give him my regards," Ernie said.

"I will," my father said.

"I'll remind him if he forgets," I added.

"How do you like Staten Island, Joe?" Ernie asked.

"Different. Very different. But good," I said.

Ernie smiled. We started to leave.

"Danny?" he called out.

We stopped. Ernie came up to us.

"I don't know how to say this. After 25 years working for your family. I should be telling your father directly, but you know, with his condition, I didn't want to upset him. I got a job working for Don Stevens. In Staten Island," he said.

My father was clearly hurt. Me, too, Ernie was like a member of the family.

"I'm sorry, Danny. I have a family. I have..." he tried to get the words out.

My father raised his hand to stop him.

"It's okay, Ernie, you don't have to explain, a man has to take care of his family. That comes before everything else. I speak for my father when I say thank you for all your years of hard work. I wish you all the luck in the world," he said, meaning every single word.

"And thank you, Danny. And thank your father for hiring me when no one else was willing to take a chance on a black man," Ernie said.

They shook hands. Ernie then turned to me and faked a punch. I didn't move. I was too sad to move. We stood there looking at Ernie getting in his pickup truck and driving off. We sensed it was the end of an era.

We headed home. Each of us downcast about the news. Wondering how my grandfather was going to take it. He was in the backyard picking grapes.

"Hey, Pop," my father said.

My grandfather nodded and continued to pick grapes.

"The Grosso job is complete. We're out of there as of today," my father informed him.

"Good. That's good," he said. "Joey, hold this basket for me."

He handed a basket over to me. I was waiting for my father to give the news. He was hesitating, waiting for the proper moment. Finally, he blurted out:

"Ernie got a job with Stevens in Staten Island," he said.

My grandfather stopped picking. You could see he was hurt.

"I'm sure when the men find out they'll be going, too. I'm sorry, Pop," my father said.

"I'm sorry, too, Grandpa."

My grandfather took the news in all too quickly like gulping a dose of bad tasting medicine to kill the taste. He went back to picking grapes.

"Tell Gina I want her to call that Chinese agent. Please," he said.

"Sure, Pop," my father said. "End of an era."

And that as they say was that.

I still had a few more weeks before I had to start school. I was getting so much experience driving. I learned how to drive from my old house to Coney Island Hospital where my grandfather was receiving his chemotherapy treatments. I was driving both him and my father one time. They were talking to each other and I felt like a fly on the wall. The way a real chauffeur must feel when his clients spoke between themselves.

"Mr. Lee called, wanted to know if we could move up the close a few days so his demolition men can start," my father said.

"Whatever you think, Danny. It's fine with me," my grandfather answered.

Then a long moment and my grandfather said what was on his mind. He talked personal. The first time I could remember him doing so. He let his guard down, showed his vulnerable side. Nearing the end of his life there was no point in putting on airs. He had entered the no spin zone.

"I feel like a failure, Danny. I feel like I failed everybody. You, Joey. My father, his father," my grandfather said.

"Come on, Pop, don't talk like that. You should be proud. You ran a good, honest business, that employed a lot of good men," my father said.

My grandfather wasn't convinced.

"Hold on, Pop. Joey pull over," my father instructed.

My father wanted to change seats with me. He wanted to drive around without telling me how to go. I put on my right turn signal and pulled over to the curb. The first thing my father did was make a gigantic, illegal U-turn. Hey, I thought, what the hell was that? But he didn't say anything. He headed toward Bay Ridge. Next thing I knew we were parked on the street in front of a beautifully detailed brownstone.

"This was the building I first helped you out on. I was ten. Ma said I was too young. But you said, "What too young? Angela, he's gotta learn," my father said.

"That sounds like me," my grandfather said.

"I showed up after school, you handed me a broom and dustpan and said, "Okay, Danny, clean up that mess." Remember what I said?"

"I only clean up messes I make," my grandfather said.

"Right. But I cleaned up that day and every day after that for a month. Then when I turned sixteen you taught me how to use tools. I'd watch every move you made. So sure. So skilled. I'd take my friends to see the buildings we worked on. All over Brooklyn," my father said.

"Really?" my grandfather asked.

"And I'd brag. My father did that. And this one, too. I couldn't have been prouder. I'm still proud. And you should be, too. And that's what a family never loses," my father said.

I could see my grandfather was beginning to feel better.

"So, don't tell me you failed the family. I won't hear of it. You listening?"

I didn't know if my grandfather was listening, but I was. And I was never prouder of being in this family.

"Take me home, Danny," he said.

A week passed and the big day had arrived. The close of escrow. I finally understood what that meant. The day my grandfather would sign the papers transferring the property to Mr. Lee's client. I was helping my grandfather find a suit to wear on this special day. My grandmother brought out a few for him to try on.

"This is the one you wore at our wedding," she said. Nope too small.

"Okay, how about this one? When Joey received his communion," she asked.

Nope too big. I looked in the closet myself and pulled out one that was in the far-right corner. Covered with, what else, clear plastic left over from the couch. I took the suit out.

"That's the suit my father wore when he came to America," my grandfather said, almost teary eyed.

I helped him put on the suit jacket. It fit perfectly. Well almost perfectly the sleeves were too long but zip zip my grandmother could fix that. She started pinning the sleeves to the correct length.

"Thank you, Angela," my grandfather said.

"For what? Fixing a suit?" she said.

"No, for putting up with me all these years," he said.

"I led the life I chose. I have no regrets," she said.

"But the vacation? The dancers?" my grandfather asked.

"There's still time for that. Plenty of time," she said.

All done. He looked in the full-length mirror hanging on the wall.

"I look just like him," my grandfather said.

"You do," she said. They laughed. A good laugh.

Then my grandfather went to his dresser drawer and took out two figurines of Flamenco dancers he'd been working on secretly. He presented it to my grandmother.

"In the meantime…" he said.

"They're beautiful. I don't know what to say," she said.

Then she lunged for his face and kissed him hard on the lips. I had never witnessed them kissing. It was nice. Awkward but nice. Then my father poked his head in.

"Time to go," he said.

We got to the office in no time flat. We took my mother's car. Squeezed in. A sales agreement was sitting in the center of a table. My grandmother, father, Uncle Tommy, Aunt Jenny, Mr. Lee, and his client were there. My mother handed a fountain pen to Mr. Lee's client who quickly signed. Probably afraid my grandfather would change his mind. He handed the pen back to my mother and she handed it to my grandfather.

"Aspetti!" he said.

He pulled me over to the corner of the room and got two inches from my face. Uh oh. What was this about I wondered?

"Are you sure you're okay with this?" he asked.

At that moment I was forced to look deep within myself and come up with an answer. A final answer. A final, final answer.

"I'm sure, Grandpa. I've decided I'm going to college and then I want to be a writer."

"Maybe you'll write about me?" he said.

"Maybe," I answered.

"Okay, then I'll sign the paper," he said. And he did.

Uncle Tommy popped the champagne. He started pouring glasses and handing them out. He spilled his all over himself. My grandmother already had a napkin at the ready.

My father walked up to my grandfather and looked him straight in the eye.

"Congratulations, Pop."

"You too, Danny."

My father smiled. He raised his glass in a toast.

"To my father, Vincent Palumbo. The best builder in Brooklyn."

"Here, here." Everyone clinked glasses. Even I was allowed to drink alcohol that Saturday.

The next day was Sunday. We had a glorious Sunday dinner in Brooklyn. Everyone was there. Including Uncle Sal, Bernice and baby Salvatore. Before dinner Uncle Tommy was showing my grandfather some architect drawings of a gym. Beautiful, state of the art.

"Big," my grandfather said.

"That's what people want, Pop. Space." Uncle Tommy said.

"You work the numbers?" my grandfather asked.

"Yeah, Pop. I've been working with an accountant. He helped me come up with a business plan," Uncle Tommy said.

My grandfather was clearly impressed.

"That's good, Tommy. You know about gyms. And you have a big heart. People will respond to that," my grandfather said.

Tommy was beaming. Then he got dead serious.

"Pop, I'm not kidding myself. You did this. Everything here is because of you. Your talent and hard work. I won't forget that," Uncle Tommy said.

Then Uncle Tommy gave my grandfather a big man hug. And my grandfather hugged him back.

My Dad then told a story I had never heard before.

"I was headed for a work detail cleaning up after our unit went through. There were four other guys, two from Brooklyn. An inseparable pair. We were driving in an old supply truck. A shoebox on wheels. We stopped and were hesitating about getting out and doing the work when the Brooklyn guys spot a huge ant hill rising up right in front of the truck. Immediately they dashed out of the truck and made a bee line towards the ant hill. Without saying a word, they began kicking the ant mound until it was totally leveled. Then they came back to the truck and one of them says to the other, "Damn, I never seen one of them before." "Me neither."

Everyone cracked up laughing, my grandfather the most.

"Yeah, that's Brooklyn alright," he said.

We went on to eat that day. We laughed, told stories, my father was holding court. He talked about Vietnam. His battle with trauma fading. That turned out to be the last Sunday dinner we had together.

A few weeks passed after we sold the property. My grandfather kept losing weight. He'd get on the scale and I'd tell him what he weighed. I'd lie. He knew by then. But it was something we did. Then one day my grandfather was too weak to get on the scale. He was in bed most of the time now. The time was near. A priest came to give him his last rites. After the priest left, I sat down alongside my grandfather. My father stayed at the door.

"Who is it?" he wanted to know.

"It's me, Joey," I said.

He opened his eyes.

"Where am I?" he asked.

"At home," I said.

"I'm tired, Joey."

"I know, Grandpa, I know. It's okay," I said.

"You're going to grow up to be a good writer," he said.

"Thanks, Grandpa."

"Remember you need a good subject to be a good writer."

"I know, Grandpa. You rest now," I said.

He closed his eyes. I motioned for my father to come over. He sat down on the bed also. He held my grandfather's right hand; I held his left. My father motioned to the rest of the family at the door. They all came in. I noticed my grandmother wasn't there. I ran outside in the hall. She was standing there. Not ready to say goodbye. I took her arm and led her into the room. To his bed. Then we all left the room and left her alone with my grandfather.

My grandfather died at home. The whole family was there. We had the wake at Graziano's Funeral Home. My grandfather's body was in an open casket. He had lost a lot of weight by then but still you knew it was him. By his hands. Everyone came. Bill and Rosemary, all the relatives, some friends, business associates. Even the Giambos. Becky and Howie came also. They were a couple now. But that was okay. They expressed their condolences and left. Holding hands. Uncle Sal was there, sobbing uncontrollably the whole time.

"He was the real thing, Joey. If I was one tenth the man your grandfather was, I'd be happy," he said, meaning every word.

"Me, too," I said.

We both had a good cry. A good manly cry.

We held the mass at St. A's. A closed casket rested in the center aisle. A large gathering. My mother sang 'Ave Maria' from the balcony. Uncle Joe accompanied her on his violin. Beautiful. He was wearing a suit that day.

Uncle Frankie came too. His Madonna and Child painting was displayed. It was finished. Finally. At the end of the ceremony we stood by the casket. Six pallbearers. My father, Uncle Sal, and Ernie, on one side, and me, Uncle Tommy, and Uncle Frankie on the other. On three we lifted his body up and carried him out. A priest splashed holy water over the casket as we left the church. An Irish priest. But nobody cared. We sat for a while waiting to drive to the Washington Cemetery. I was in the front limo with my grandmother, father, mother, and Uncle Tommy. I turned around to see the long line of cars with their headlights on.

"Gee, Dad, Grandpa was big," I remarked.

"Yeah, Joey, he was big," my father said.

We got the signal and our driver pulled out. Mike the cop was our police escort. We all gathered at his grave. Lots of crying. A priest said a few words and they lowered my grandfather's body into his grave.

After the funeral we went on with our lives. Aunt Jenny and Rudy got married in New Mexico. The whole family was there. They came from all over, Brooklyn, Staten Island, Long Island and Florida. Aunt Jenny and Rudy, the happy bride and groom danced all night. So did Aunt Theresa and Uncle Frankie. Aunt Theresa wore a red dress for the occasion. Uncle Tommy was wearing a white 'Tommy's Gym' T-shirt. It had a red burgundy stain tie dyed on it. Uncle Sal and Bernice danced with baby Sal. I just watched. I didn't want to miss a thing.

I wound up going to Brooklyn College. I stayed with my grandmother at the old house. I majored in Creative writing. I moved to Northern California got married and had two terrific kids. I built spec houses. In my spare time I wrote. Screenplays, spec sitcoms. At forty-five years old I moved down to Hollywood to write on the acclaimed TV show Brooklyn Bridge. I was hired by Gary David Goldberg, a Jewish friend from Brooklyn. My mother told me to hang around the Jewish kids they were going places. She was right!

The End

GLOSSARY

ITALIAN	ENGLISH
Aspetti!	Wait!
Boccalone	Talks a lot
Capisce?	Understand?
Cidrule	Big Dope
Potz	Crazy
Zitellona	Old maid

YIDDISH	ENGLISH
Boychik	Young boy
Bubellah	Anyone you like
Chutzpah	Brazenness
Plotz	Burst
Schlep	Drag
Shvitz	Sweat

ARABIC	ENGLISH
Ya Allah	Oh my God
Dib	Dope
Eckle	To eat
Sully	Remember to pray
Rhoohi	Sweet darling
Gee bah	Go get it

MARTHA'S ITALIAN MARINARA SAUCE

1/2 cup extra virgin olive oil

2 small onions, finely chopped

3 cloves of garlic, finely chopped

1/2 teaspoon sea salt

1/2 teaspoon freshly ground pepper

2 32 ounce cans crushed tomatoes

1/2 teaspoon of basil

In a large casserole pot heat the oil over a medium-high flame. Add the onions and garlic and sauté until the onions are translucent. Add 1/2 teaspoon each of salt and pepper. Add the tomatoes and basil and simmer uncovered over low heat until the sauce thickens, about an hour. Season the sauce with more salt and pepper to taste.

INVITE THE FAMILY OVER!
BUONO APPETITO!

THE END END